The Tippler's Touring Guide to Wales

Clive Williams

An Imbiber's Guide to Camping, Touring and Motor Caravanning Sites

Campsites – Attractions – Out and About – Pubs

23 Selected Campsites + Pubs Galore to Visit and Enjoy!

Detailed information on the sites – facilities – location – directions, etc.

Local information and history – places to go – things to do – sights to see.

Easy to follow directions from the campsites to the pubs – a kind of A to B directory.

Easy to follow alphabetic cataloguing system.

Full of facts and figures without frills and fancies.

The essential companion for the dedicated camper who enjoys a drink to round off the day – with directions to the pubs that no sat-nav can possibly give!

Introduction

As one who enjoys a pint and good company to round off a perfect day 'out and about', I always endeavour to seek out a campsite that is within a sensible walking distance of a hostelry serving fine ale. Being a keen walker, my idea of a 'sensible' distance is anything up to one and a half miles, as anything more than this turns the evening into a marathon!

Lack of knowledge on the whereabouts of good pubs has often frustrated me, as this kind of information does not tend to appear in caravan and camping guides. So in writing this guide I am setting out to help fellow imbibers enjoy their touring trips around our beautiful country, as well as providing them with a little local knowledge about my chosen locations.

The book is not intended to be an in-depth guide but rather to whet your appetite and encourage you to use your spirit of adventure to seek out 'The Wonders of Wales' for yourself.

I have been very selective in choosing the campsites, so that you will not be disappointed with them or with their locations. After all, they have to be the kind of sites that I like to visit!

I have also been very selective in choosing the pubs, inns and hotels that I have included, and they have all been tried and tested by me. Again, they have to be the kind of hostelries that I like to visit! To assist you in enjoying your evenings out after your hard day's adventures I have provided easy to follow directions from the campsites to the pubs – a kind of A to B directory.

Most important of all, the book is aimed at helping you get the most out of your touring adventure and be able to relax at the end of the day with that well deserved pint!

As they say in Wales ~ Iechyd da!

As they say in Ireland ~ Sláinte mhaith!
As they say in Scotland ~ Slàinte mhath!

Good health!

Please be aware that great care has been taken in compiling this guide and the information it contains is as accurate as possible at the time of publishing; unfortunately any subsequent changes are beyond my control.

Clive Williams y Silwrydd/the Silurist
Aberbargod/Aberbargoed
Cymru/Wales
2017

The Tippler's Touring Guide to Ireland

The Tippler's Touring Guide to Scotland

The Tippler's Touring Guide to Wales

Contents

Index of Locations and Names of Campsites

Map of Wales Showing the Locations

From Aberaeron to Trearddur Bay

Locations and Campsites A-Z

A. ABERAERON

Aeron Coast Caravan Park
North Road
Aberaeron
Ceredigion
SA46 0JF
Tel: 01545 570349
Fax: 01545 571289
www.aeroncoast.co.uk
Email: enquiries@aeroncoast.co.uk

Open: March to October

Pitches for: There are 200 owner occupied static caravans. The remainder of the plots have been developed to accommodate up to 100 touring caravans, motorized homes and tents.

Acreage: The 8 acre Park is set within 22 acres of flat coastal land on Cardigan Bay.

Access: Good

Site location: Level. The Park is set within 22 acres of flat coastal land on Cardigan Bay only 200 yards from picturesque harbour and shops. Quiet out of season but good facilities for children during school summer holidays. Caravan holiday homes are privately owned and not for letting.

Facilities: There are two conveniently placed large toilet blocks with showers and free hot water. Both blocks have washing up areas and disposal points. There is a laundry room with two industrial-size washing machines and tumble dryer.

There are special facilities for the disabled and a baby changing room.

All pitches are clearly marked with electric hook ups.

The Office is available to supply any extra information or help you might need. It sells Calor gas and has a wide range of leaflets with ideas as to how you might explore this beautiful part of Wales. There is a public telephone box outside the Office and emergency telephone numbers are posted here. For a quick convenience shop, the Petrol Station at the entrance of the Park has a good selection of essentials.

There is a Club House which all adults automatically join when they book in. The Club offers a large open plan lounge, separate family room and television room. Children under the age of 16 years are not permitted in some areas of the Club after 9pm. The Club offers bar meals and take away snacks at lunchtime and in the evenings after 6.30pm at the weekends, bank holidays and school holidays.

Attached to the Club House is a leisure complex with an under 5's room, table tennis, air hockey and two pool rooms.

The Aeron Room is the venue for evening entertainment with seating for 150. During school holidays, a resident entertainer organizes family events which are listed on notice boards around the Park. They range from discos, games, quiz nights and films to fancy dress competitions and talent contests. On Saturday nights in the main part of the season and peak periods there are evening events which include live professional artists and themed evenings. Entertainment is free of charge and informal.

Outdoor facilities include an enclosed complex of three heated outdoor swimming pools, one of these being a paddling pool for the youngest swimmers. There are sun loungers and tables with parasols. The pools and poolside area are unsupervised and patrons are urged to accompany any child under 15 to the pool area and be aware of the safety notices and life saving equipment.

At the far end of the Park are full-size and half-size tennis courts together with a hard-surface 5 a-side football/basketball area and a large sandpit with Pirate Ship.

Dogs are welcome. There is a dog walking area. Due to safety, dogs are not allowed to wander on the Park and must be kept on leads at all times. Any owner abusing this will be asked to leave. Dogs must not be walked by children under 12 years.

Nearby facilities: Golf, fishing, sailing, boating, horse riding, water skiing, tennis.

Rates: On application

Directions: Main A487 coastal road. Northern edge of Aberaeron. Brown sign-posting. Filling Station at entrance.

Nearest town/resort: Aberaeron

Out and about: Aberaeron is a recognised beauty spot - an ideal family holiday location with safe bathing on the nearby beach. Other nearby seaside locations worth a visit are Llanon and Llanrhystud to the north, and New Quay, Llangrannog and Aberporth to the south. A visit to the sea aquarium on the quay is a must, and while you are still on the quay why not treat yourself to a delicious locally made ice cream flavoured with honey. Take a stroll along the banks of the River Aeron or just sit on Alban Square and watch the world go by. Aberaeron is the perfect place to unwind (and the fish and chips are excellent!). Take a trip into the hinterland, via the A482 to the market town of Lampeter, home of St. David's College. From there take the A485 to Tregaron, birthplace of Thomas Jones, better known as the notorious Twm Sion Catti - he lived by plundering his neighbours, amassed a fortune by marrying an heiress by means of a trick, and was later appointed High Sheriff of the county. Then take the B4343 to Pontrhydfendigaid. About 1 mile east of this typically Welsh village you will discover the peaceful remains of Strata Florida Abbey. The Church of St. Mary stands in the grounds of the abbey; and here, beneath a large yew tree in the churchyard, you will find the alleged burial place of the famous 14th century poet, Dafydd ap Gwilym.

The pub, A to B: Leave the Park by way of the small gate at the rear in the bottom far left corner. A pleasant 400 yards stroll along the seafront will bring you into Aberaeron, a pretty Georgian town blessed with an abundance of hotels and pubs. The first you will encounter is The Harbourmaster Hotel on your left on Quay Parade, which, as its name suggests, overlooks the harbour. Further along Quay Parade and to the left around the corner in Market Street, facing the harbour, is my favourite - *The Cadwgan Inn - Tafarn y Cadwgan* - with its cosy, friendly atmosphere - I'm sure you will find it most pleasing! And then there are The Monachty Hotel and The Castle Hotel, both in Market Street; plus a few more scattered about the town for you to visit. Not forgetting, of course, The Royal Oak on North Road. To get there, turn left after the Castle Hotel on the corner and walk along to Alban Square. The Royal Oak is on your right just past Alban Square near to the main entrance to Aeron Coast.

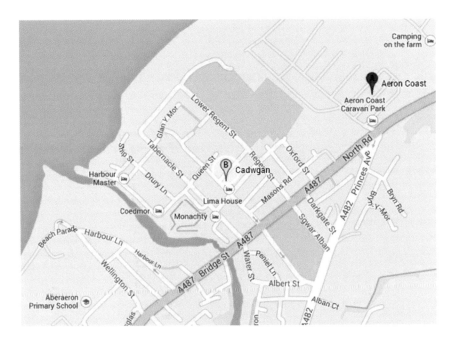

A. Aeron Coast to B. The Cadwgan Inn/Tafarn y Cadwgan

B. ABERYSTWYTH

Aberystwyth Holiday Village
Penparcau Road
Aberystwyth
Ceredigion
SY23 1TH
Tel: 01970 624211
Fax: 01970 611536
www.aberystwyth-holidays.co,uk
Email: enquiries@aberystwythholidays.co.uk

Open: March to October

Pitches for: Aberystwyth Holiday Village accommodates up to 500 tents, tourers and motorhomes plus 200 static holiday homes.

Acreage: The 16 acre Caravan and Camping field is set within the 30 acres of Aberystwyth Holiday Village.

Access: Good

Site location: Totally flat site. Just a few minutes' walk from Aberystwyth town centre and beach. Ideal for a family holiday or an overnight stay.

Facilities: There is a choice of tarmac or grass pitches, many of which have electric hook-up points. All pitches are close to modern shower and toilet facilities which are open 24 hours. All showers are free. Pitches are available from 1 night to a complete season.

You can enjoy an extensive range of on-site facilities, including:
Indoor Heated Swimming Pool
Fitness Centre
Sun Beds
Ten Pin Bowling Centre
Amusements – Bingo
Restaurant
Fast Food Takeaway
Lounge Bar (Children Welcome)
Family Entertainment Bar
Mini-market/Gift Shop
Caravan Accessory Shop
On Park Fishing
Children's Play Area
Free Wi-Fi

During peak season (School Summer Holidays) and Bank Holiday Weekends you can enjoy live entertainment every night in the large family entertainment bar. You can dance every night to the resident DJ or to a band. There is children's entertainment to keep them happy. Each week there are top comedians, singers, dancers and magic shows. There is also a Lounge Bar for those who want to relax in a quieter atmosphere.

Private caravan hire is available. Please note that Aberystwyth Holiday Village does not hire any caravans. All caravans for hire are privately owned. 2/3 bedroom fully equipped caravans are available to hire from Easter - 31st October for an overnight stay or a full holiday. A list of owners that hire their caravans out is available on the Holiday Village's website. Please call them direct for prices, availability and full details. When hiring a privately owned caravan prices will vary due to caravan size, quality and service provided by the caravan owner. All facilities are free when hiring privately owned caravans.

Dogs are welcome. Most types or dogs are allowed, however pitbulls, staffs, dobermans, rottweillers or any cross breed of this type are not.

Nearby facilities: Golf, fishing, sailing, tennis, beach, town with shops and restaurants, and much more.

Rates: On application

Directions: ½ mile south east of Aberystwyth on the A487.

Nearest town/resort: Aberystwyth

Out and about: Aberystwyth, 'the cultural capital of Wales', is home to the National Library of Wales and is also the seat of local and some national government departments; a university centre, and home to numerous national bodies, as well as an important shopping focus. It is worth taking a trip on the Vale of Rheidol narrow gauge line to Devil's Bridge to take in the magnificent scenery. Another fine experience is a ride on the funicular railway to the top of Constitution Hill where the observatory is located. A walk along the graceful crescent shaped promenade is also worthwhile – take in the flags flying from the flagpoles – they represent European nations whose languages are (unfortunately) regarded as 'minority languages'; but alive nonetheless! The castle, whose ruins are laid out as gardens form a viewpoint for sitting and looking out over Cardigan Bay. Ceredigion Museum will also give you an insight into the town's and surrounding district's history and heritage

The pub, A to B: Turn right out of The Holiday Village down the hill through Trefechan and over the bridge. Carry straight ahead up Bridge Street and you will find The Nag's Head on your left. It's less than half a mile from the Holiday Village so you shouldn't be too exhausted at this point.
A little further up Bridge Street on your right is Yr Hen Lew Du. Just a little further up the street is the junction with Great Dark Street. You are now in the centre of the town where you will find an abundance of welcoming taverns, amongst them Downies Vaults in Eastgate, The Ship and Castle in High Street, The Angel Inn in Great Darkgate Street, The Vale of Rheidol on Terrace Road and The Pier Hotel in Pier Street.
Now, if you are feeling energetic enough, a walk down Great Dark Street along North Parade with Aber Vaults on your right in Thespian Street, and on along Northgate Street to the bottom of Penglais Road and the junction of Llanbadarn Road and you

are there! The warm and friendly *Coopers Arms* on Northgate Street, better known as *The Coops or Y Cŵps - Aber's finest!*

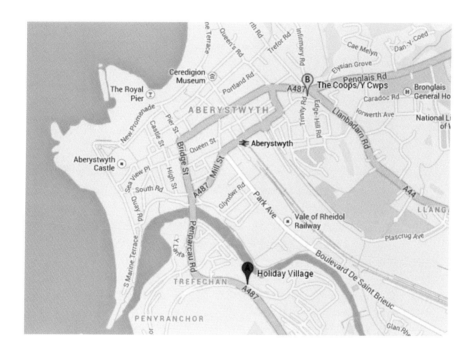

A. Holiday Village to B. The Coopers Arms/Y Cŵps

C. BALA

Pen y Bont Touring Park
Llangynog Road
Bala
Gwynedd
LL23 7PH
Tel: 01678 520549
Fax: 01678 520006
www.penybont-bala.co.uk
Email: penybont-bala@btconnect.com

Open: Mid March to late October

Pitches for: The Park has been developed to accommodate a combination of 95 Touring Caravan, Motor Home and Tent pitches.

Acreage: The Caravan and Campsite itself covers 6 acres and has been sensitively landscaped with the pitches intermingled with trees.

Access: Good

Site location: Pen y Bont is situated 100 yards from Bala Lake, Bala lake Railway and is ¾ of a mile to Bala town centre along a flat paved footpath. The Park is set in beautiful natural surroundings and has been sensitively landscaped to accommodate the natural lay of the land. The land is gently sloping in parts and flat in others.

Facilities:

Camping:

16 amp electrical hook-up available for a number of tent pitches.
Free hot showers.
Under Cover Food Preparation/Washing up area.
Disabled/Family Toilet + Shower Facilities - baby bath + changing mat etc.
Fully Equipped Laundry.
Hair Dryers and separate plug point for own use.
Chemical Disposal Point.
24hr Telephone.
Wi-Fi
Battery/Lap Top and Phone Charging available.
Security of CCTV.
Drinking water points situated throughout the Park.
Freezer/Ice Block service.
Well stocked shop selling essentials - camping accessories - Calor Gas

Motor Home:

All Motor Home pitches have electrical hook-up, some having water and drainage.
Motor Home Service Point

Free hot showers.
Under Cover Food Preparation/Washing up area.
Disabled/Family Toilet + Shower Facilities - baby bath + changing mat etc.
Fully Equipped Laundry.
Hair Dryers and separate plug point for own use.
Chemical Disposal Point.
24hr Telephone.
Wi-Fi
Battery/Lap Top and Phone Charging available.
Security of CCTV.
Drinking water points situated throughout the Park.
Well stocked shop selling, essentials - camping accessories - Calor Gas
Winter & Summer Storage - Details on Request.

Caravan:

All Caravan pitches have 16 amp electrical hook-up, some having water and drainage.
Electrical hook-up also available for a number of tent pitches.
Free hot showers.
Under Cover Food Preparation/Washing up area.
Disabled/Family Toilet + Shower Facilities - baby bath + changing mat etc.
Fully Equipped Laundry.
Hair Dryers and separate plug point for own use.
Chemical Disposal Point.
24hr Telephone.
Wi-Fi
Battery/Lap Top and Phone Charging available.
Security of CCTV.
Drinking water points situated throughout the Park.
Freezer/Ice Block service.
Winter & Summer Storage - Details on Request.

Dogs are welcome. Don't leave your dogs at home the site is Pet Friendly, they are part of your family and welcome on the park, they must however be kept on a lead or secured whilst on the park itself, though there are plenty of great dog walks just around the corner.

Nearby facilities: Golf, fishing, sailing, boating, horse riding, tennis, climbing.

Rates: On application

Directions: ½ mile south of Bala on the B4391. (If you are travelling from the South and using the postcode for satnav purposes, please be mindful that the satnav doesn't take you over the Berwyn Mountains as the roads are too narrow and winding for towing and driving large vehicles - it would be wise to follow the A5 route).

Nearest town/resort: Bala

Out and about: Bala Lake, or Llyn Tegid, is located on the western side of the town. It is the largest natural lake in Wales, and home to the Gwyniad, a fish found nowhere else in the world (a fine stuffed specimen is displayed in The Royal White Lion Hotel). Bala Lake Railway runs along the southern shore of the lake as far as Llanuwchlyn. It was to Bala that Mary Jones, aged sixteen, made her epic walk, barefoot most of the way to save her shoes, across the mountains from her home at Llanfihangel y Pennant to purchase a bible from Thomas Charles. This impressed Charles so much that it inspired him to found The British and Foreign Bible Society. His statue stands near Capel Tegid in Tegid Street. There are breathtaking views of the mountains of Arenig Fawr, Aran Benllyn and Aran Fawddwy.

The pub, A to B: A gentle ½ mile stroll from the Park will bring you to Bala town with its numerous selection of hotels and pubs. As you leave the Park turn to your left and walk down the road and straight ahead across the bridge over the River Dee. 100 yards after the bridge branch off left into Tegid Street and follow along into the town centre. Where Tegid Street meets Stryd Fawr you will see The White Lion Royal Hotel straight across the road in front of you – why not pop in to see the stuffed Gwyniad and enjoy a drink at the same time! On leaving The White Lion, turn to your left, and walk just a short way along Stryd Fawr to The Goat Hotel. Crossing the road in front of The Goat, turning to your right, and walking a fairly short distance in the other direction along Stryd Fawr will bring you to *Ye Olde Bulls Head* – a welcoming pub with a good range of real ales.

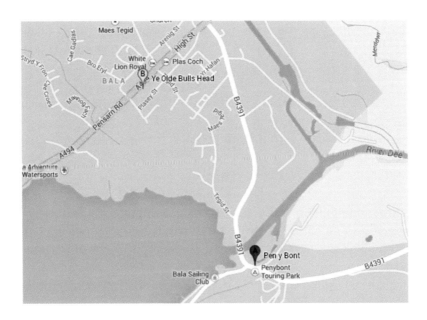

A. Pen y Bont to B. Ye Olde Bulls Head

D. BEDDGELERT

Cae Du Campsite

Beddgelert
Gwynedd
LL55 4NE
Tel: 01766 890345
www.caeducampsite.co.uk
Email: stay@caeducampsite.co.uk

*For bookings and information call **between10.00 and 18.00***
Urgent calls accepted outside these hours.

Open: Late March to end September.

Pitches for: Cae Du can accommodate up to 25 touring caravans and dormobiles and up to 85 tents.

Acreage: A spacious site of 30 acres set on the banks of the river Glaslyn.

Access: Good

Site location: This is a peaceful caravan and camping site on the river Glaslyn at the edge of Beddgelert in the heart of the Snowdonia National Park. It is an ideal location for exploring the mountains of Snowdonia and the coastline and attractions of North Wales for those seeking a quiet relaxing camping break or holiday.

Facilities: There are modern, purpose built clean facilities including toilets, hot showers and dishwashing facilities:
hot showers and washbasins
shaving points
power points on meter
dishwashing facilities
chemical toilet disposal point
laundry facilities

Electric hook-ups are available.

There are fishing rights on the river Glaslyn passing through the site.

Dogs are welcome. Dogs are to be kept on a lead on the site.

Nearby facilities: Beddgelert, with its shops and places to eat, is just a few minutes' walk away. There plenty of walks from the campsite including the peaks of Snowdon, Moel Hebog and Cnicht, or more leisurely valley walks. Mountain bikes can be hired from Beddgelert Bikes. There are many attractions within easy reach of the campsite including Sygun Copper Mine; castles at Caernarvon and Criccieth; Portmeirion; and the steam railways of the Snowdon Mountain Railway, Welsh Highland Railway and Ffestiniog Railway.

Rates: On application

Directions: Cae Du is ½ mile northeast of Beddgelert on the A498 Nantgwynant road. The Campsite can be approached from the A55 North Wales Expressway via Bangor and Caernarfon, or from the A5 via Bettws y Coed.

Nearest town/resort: Beddgelert

Out and about: This is the perfect location for touring the Snowdonia National Park with its endless attractions too numerous to list in full. Fantastic scenery, walks, fishing – are all on the doorstep. Beddgelert translates into English as 'Gelert's grave'. Discover the sad story about Gelert, favourite hound of Llywelyn the Great, and visit his grave in the meadow by the river. Walk or drive through the magnificent Aberglaslyn Pass. Go down Sygun copper mine. Climb Moel Hebog. Take a trip shopping in nearby Caernarfon, Porthmadog or Bettws y Coed. Visit one of the majestic castles for which the area is famous. Take the train (the easy way!) to the summit of Snowdon. Or simply soak up the ambience of this beautiful village cradled in the heart of the mountains. You will be hard pushed to find a more idyllic spot!

The pub, A to B: From the Campsite walk the 500 yards to the main road and turn to your left in the direction of Beddgelert which is another 500 yards away. There's an alternative way to the main road from the back of the Campsite, but it isn't really any shorter. There are four well-appointed hostelries in the village - all waiting to welcome you! The Prince Llewelyn is on one side of the bridge in Stryd Smith, and The Saracen's Head can be found on the same side of the bridge as 'The Prince', only a little further along on the A4085 (Caernarfon Road). The (local) family run *Tanronnen* is on the other side of the bridge on the A498 (Porthmadog Road), and the The Royal Goat Hotel can be reached on the same side of the bridge as 'The Tan', only just up the road at the edge of the village.

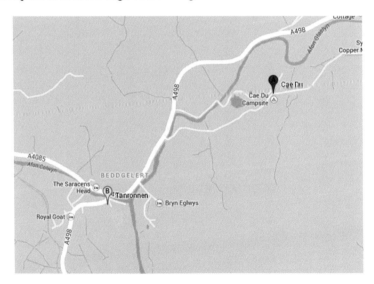

A. Cae Du to B. the Tanronnen

E. BODFARI

Station House Caravan Park
Bodfari
Denbigh
Denbighshire
LL16 4DA
Tel: 01745 710372
www.stationhousecaravanpark.co.uk
Email: email@stationhousecaravanpark.co.uk

Open: Easter/April to October

Pitches for: Station House has 26 level touring pitches for tents, touring caravans and motor caravans.

Acreage: The 2 acre Park is very well landscaped, being grassed, level, firm and well drained.

Site location: Built in the 1860's; Station House served as Bodfari Railway Station, until the line was closed under the Beeching Plan in 1962. A quiet friendly Caravan Park, in beautiful countryside, situated on the western edge of the attractive village of Bodfari. There are superb views in all directions from the Park, with Moel y Park and Moel Arthur the dominating features, with the famous Offa's Dyke Path only 350 yards away. The Park is located on the A541 Mold to Denbigh road, some 3½ miles north east of Denbigh. Within easy reach of the A55 expressway, the Park is very convenient as a centre for touring the North Wales Coast, Snowdonia and the whole of the North East of Wales. The Ordinance Survey Map Reference is SJ 095699 and is on sheet 116 of the most useful, Land Ranger Series 1:50,000.

Facilities: The excellent site facilities include:
Toilet block with shower
Washing up area
Water points
Chemical toilet disposal
Electrical Hook Up Points
Gas Bottle Exchange
Battery Charging

Dogs are welcome. Dogs must be kept on a leash and exercised off the Park.

Nearby facilities: The village shop (with Link cash facilities) and the village inn are both within ¼ mile of the park. Walking, fishing, sailing, swimming, pony trekking and golf are some of the many activities available within a ten mile radius of the park and much less in several instances.

Rates: On application

Directions: The recommended route to the Park is by turning off the A541 (Mold – Denbigh Road), in the village of Bodfari, onto the B5429 in the direction of Tremeirchion. The Park entrance is on the left, only 40 yards after leaving the A541, at a cream house. Using the B5429 from the A55 is not recommended.

Nearest town/resort: Denbigh

Out and about: Situated in the Vale of Clwyd, the Park is central for touring North East Wales. Denbigh with its 13th century castle is only 3 miles to the south-west. St. Asaph, which has the smallest cathedral in Wales is only 6 miles away to the north, and a little further on is Rhuddlan with its 13th century castle. A short journey further north brings you to the coastal towns of Rhyl and Prestatyn. If you are looking for a 'lively' time these are the places to be! The Marble Church (St. Margaret's Church), Bodelwyddan, is a prominent landmark in the lower Vale of Clwyd is visible for many miles. Here are the graves of Canadian soldiers, some of whom are believed to have died during mutinous riots at the Kinmel Bay military camp in March 1919. Ruthin, the old county town of Denbighshire, with its castle that dates back to 1281, lies to the south. Ruthin Goal is well worth a visit (but not, I would add, for a long-term stay). And also whilst in the town you can step back into seven ages of history at Wales' oldest timbered town house at Nantclwyd y Dre. The Clwydian Hills, which dominate the region, are well worth exploring and an ascent of Moel Famau will provide magnificent views of the region. Visitors of all faiths or of none at all are made welcome at St. Winefride's Well at Holywell on Deeside, to share its unique mixture of history, beauty and peace. Wrexham, 20 miles to the south-east, boasts one of the 'Seven Wonders of Wales'; the parish church of St. Giles, with its magnificent 136 foot high tower. Llangollen, home to the Internation Eisteddfod, lies 25 miles away to the south and can be reached via the spectacular Horseshoe Pass on the A542. The majestic ruins of Valle Crucis Abbey can be viewed on route. Perched high on its hilltop the romantic ruins of Castell Dinas Bran overlook the picturesque town. In Llangollen itself, you can visit Plas Newydd, which was home to 'The Ladies of Llangollen', two eccentric spinsters who escaped here from the conventions of Irish society in the eighteenth century. Four miles east of Llangollen Thomas Telford's Pontcysyllte Aqueduct carries the Llangollen Canal high above the deep ravine of the river Dee.

The pub, A to B: Bodfari used to boast two public houses, but sadly the Dinorben Arms has since closed. The *Downing Arms* however; is still open! Turn right out of the Park then left at the main road and walk the short distance along the A541 in the direction of Mold to Downing's – a real village pub where you are sure of a warm welcome and a good pint of ale!

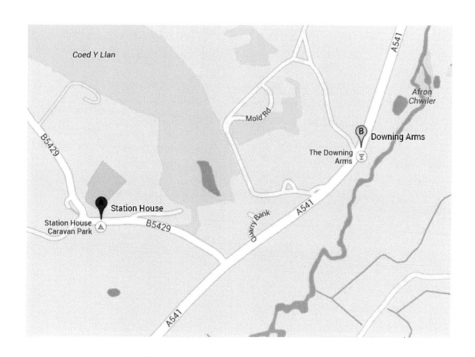

A. Station House to B. the Downing Arms

F. BUILTH WELLS

White House Camp Site
Hay Road
Builth Wells
Powys
LD2 3BP
Tel: 01982 552255 *(but please only call **during office hours** (9am – 5pm Monday to Friday)*
www.whitehousecampsite.co.uk
Email: info@whitehousecampsite.co.uk

Open: April to October

Pitches for: The Camp Site has 30 touring pitches for tents, touring caravans and motor caravans, with hard standing pitches and electric hook ups.

Acreage: The entire 2½ acre site is flat and level.

Access: Good

Site location: White House Campsite is a small caravan and camping site in the Heart of Wales. The Site is right next to the River Wye and only a short walk to the centre of Builth Wells and the Royal Welsh Showground at Llanelwedd. It's a great place to stay for a while, with electric hook ups, hard standing pitches and hot water for washing up. The whole site is flat and level with a clean shower and toilet block designed to be accessible for people with disabilities.

Facilities: On-site facilities include:
Clean shower and toilet block designed to be accessible for people with disabilities
Hot water for washing up
Electric hook ups
Hard standing pitches
Chemical toilet disposal

Dogs are welcome

White House Caravan and Camping Site Accessibility Statement:

We are fully committed to being disability friendly at White House Camping and Caravan Site.

The site is situated on a level field adjacent to the River Wye.

A level 130m well lit road, part tarmacadam, part tarred gravel, leaves the A470 trunk road and leads to the site.

Access to the town of Builth Wells (approx. 300 metres) is by street pavement with appropriate dropped kerbs for wheelchair access.

Pitches are grass or hard standing, with space for awnings on hard standing or grass surfaces.

Parking besides your caravan or tent is allowed.

Internal roads have grass or well compacted hard core surfaces.

A modern toilet block has a dedicated room (2.2m x 2.5m) with a 80cm wide outward facing door. Facilities include the usual toilet and hand basin plus a wheelchair accessible shower. Grab rails are fitted throughout this room.

Water points, chemical toilet disposal and dustbin areas are no further than 60m from any pitch.

All pitches are accessible by car.

Local bus services pass the site entrance & local taxis service the park.

Mobile telephone reception is good and there is also a coin operated telephone box approximately 300m from the site entrance.

Although we have tried to be as accurate as possible and include as much detail as we can in this statement, we are always willing to give information on any aspect of the park, if this statement does not answer your particular question.

Nearby facilities: There is plenty to keep you busy in Builth Wells including an 18-hole golf course, tennis courts, sports centre, swimming pool and good bars and restaurants. There are lots of opportunities nearby for outdoor activities including walking, fishing, and cycling. The site is on the route of the Wye Valley Walk and Lôn Las Cymru, the Welsh National Cycle Route which runs from north to south Wales.

Royal Welsh Show:
Around 400 events take place at the Showground each year. Click on the link on the White House Camp Site website *Royal Welsh Show Page* or
visit the **Royal Welsh Agricultural Society** website: www.rwas.co.uk for a list of events taking place there.

Walking:
The Wye Valley Walk passes through Builth Wells, and there are countless footpaths and bridleways in the hills of Breckonshire and Radnorshire which surround the town. The 90km Epynt Way, is a circular bridleway around the Epynt Range MOD training area.
For some other great walks around Builth Wells click on the link on the White House Camp Site *Activities Page* or visit: www.builth-wells.co.uk for more details.

Cycling:
The Campsite is at roughly the half-way point between Holyhead and Cardiff or Chepstow on Lôn Las Cymru, or National Cycle Route 8 - click on the link on the

White House Camp Site *Activities Page* or visit: www.routes2ride.org.uk for more details.

The opportunities for biking in the area are excellent, with miles of quiet country roads to be explored. See the White House Camp Site website *Cycling Page* for more details.

Fishing:

The Campsite is next to the river Wye and near to the rivers Irfon, Duhonw and Edw. The Upper Wye Passport scheme allows you to fish for wild trout and salmon on a roving voucher system and day permits for the area can be bought in town – click on the link on the White House Camp Site website *Activities Page* or visit: www.wyeuskfoundation.org for details.

There is also good course fishing on offer only seven miles away at Llandrindod Lake.

Golf:

There's an excellent 18-hole course at Builth Wells Golf Club, where the clubhouse is a converted 15th century traditional Welsh Long House. Llandrindod Wells golf course is also nearby, and both clubs are open to visitors.

Canoeing:

Canoeists can access the river Wye whenever the river is running high or at any time outside the main fishing season – click on the link on the White House Camp Site website *Activities Page* or visit: www.wyeuskfoundation.org for more details.

The Campsite is right next to the river so you can stay there for an overnight stop on the way down the river Wye and groups can be accommodated. Canoes are also available for hire at Glasbury - only a 20 minute drive (or a 15 mile paddle!) from the site – click on the link on the White House Camp Site website *Activities Page* or visit: www.wyevalleycanoes.co.uk for details.

Rugby:

Builth Wells rugby team play in Division Two of the Welsh League, and play their home matches on the Groe park. If you're heading down to Cardiff to watch a match at the Millennium Stadium, break up the journey and spend the night in Builth!

Leisure Centre & Swimming Pool:

Builth Wells Leisure Centre has two squash courts, gym, sauna and sports hall. The pool is next door - check details on 01982 552324. Click on the link on the White House Camp Site *Activities Page* or visit: www.powys.gov.uk/index.

Rates: On application

Directions: The site is on the A470 on the eastern edge of Builth Wells, 300 yards from the town centre.

By road:

A470: Approaching Builth Wells from the south, the site is the first right after the 30mph signs.

Approaching from the north, turn right at the roundabout outside the main entrance to the Royal Welsh Showground, drive over the bridge into Builth, take the first left at Wyeside Arts Centre, and the site is on your left after 200m.

A483: Approaching Builth Wells from the south, drive through Builth Wells following the one way system, go straight on at the staggered junction by the bridge and Wyeside Art Centre, and the site is 200m on your left.
Approaching from the north, turn left at the roundabout outside the main entrance to the Royal Welsh Showground, drive over the bridge into Builth, take the first left at Wyeside Arts Centre, and the site is on your left after 200m.

By train, bus or bike:
See the White House website *How to Find Us Page* for more details.

Nearest town/resort: Builth Wells

Out and about: The Royal Welsh Showground lies just across the River Wye in Llanelwedd. At Cilmery, 2½ miles west of Builth Wells on the A483, is the roadside monument to Llywelyn ap Gruffydd, last of the native Welsh princes, who was killed near this spot in 1282. See also the well where it is reputed his severed head was washed before being taken to London to be paraded around on a pole. Journey further west along the A483 to visit the Cambrian Woollen Mill at Llanwrtyd Wells where the St. David's Tartan cloth is produced, and which has an excellent gift shop.

Head up into the hills:
Turn south off the A483 at Garth, between Builth Wells and Llanwrtyd Wells, and follow the B4519 up onto Mynydd Epynt which offers stunning panoramic views of the district.
For a truly exhilarating experience take the unclassified road north-west at Beulah, between Builth Wells and Llanwrtyd Wells, which leads up through Abergwesyn, and over the empty open moors to Tregaron. The scenery here is wild and grand.

The pub, A to B: After turning right out of the Campsite and strolling leisurely along the road for 300 yards, passing the mural depicting the slaying of Llywelyn on your way, you will arrive in the town centre. Builth's main shopping highway changes its name halfway along - one part is Broad Street and the other is High Street. Here you will find four pubs in all. Firstly, on your right on Broad Street is The Fountain Inn, with The Lamb Inn more or less directly across the road. A little further along, on High Street, is the *White Horse Hotel* and The White Hart Inn just twenty or so yards after. The White Horse always appears popular with the locals, and I always enjoy the atmosphere there. Just off the centre of the town is The Greyhound Hotel on Garth Road (A483 Llandovery/Llanwrtyd Wells Road). Its beers and ales are renowned in these parts, with plenty of choice from local Welsh breweries and micro-breweries.

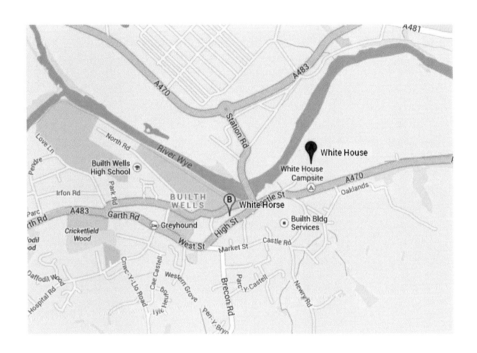

A. White House to B. the White Horse Hotel

G. CHAINBRIDGE

Pont Kemys Caravan & Camping Park
Chainbridge
Abergavenny
Monmouthshire
NP7 9DS
Tel: 01873 880688
Fax: 01873 880270
www.pontkemys.co.uk
Email: info@pontkemys.com

Open: March to October

Pitches for: The Park has 65 level touring pitches for tents, touring caravans and motor caravans.

Acreage: The site sits in 13 acres with many mature and semi mature trees in the grounds.

Access: Good

Site location: This peaceful park lies adjacent to the River Usk only eight miles from Abergavenny and four miles from the town of Usk on the B4598. It is served by an internal tarmac road and is level, well drained with many hard standings. There are 20 fully serviced pitches in an adult only area. Whilst the site is in a peaceful location, many tourist attractions and places of interest are close at hand or are easily accessible due to good road links. The ideal location for touring Monmouthshire, the Usk Valley walk, cycle route 42, the Brecon Beacons, Raglan Castle.

Facilities: Pont Kemys is a family run park which has been developed after a long association with caravanners and campers.

Here's the rundown of facilities at Pont Kemys:

Facilities block - well equipped with toilets, wash basins, showers, hand & hair dryers - all free

Adult only area - with fully serviced super-pitches (electric, drainage, direct water supply and TV connection, Wi-Fi - on a generous sized pitch)

Free Wi-Fi for all guests.
Disabled person toilet/shower room
Baby changing room
Laundry room – washer, drier and iron
Washing up room
Television lounge
All caravan pitches with electric hook ups
Reception area and shop – gas, basic provisions, weekend newspapers to order

Separate dog exercise area
Public Telephone

Please note the Park operates a recycling policy. There are containers for the following items: mixed glass, newspapers and magazines, plastic milk and pop bottles, cardboard, cans.

Dogs are welcome. The dog walk is in a separate field adjacent to the site and next to the River Usk.

Pont Kemys Caravan and Camping Park Access Policy Statement:

Site has touring caravan and tent pitches

Site reception has ample parking and access ramp

All pitches have parking alongside

Main site is level and is well serviced by flat tarmac roads. No loose/uneven road surfaces on site

Access to facilities building is by paved ramp

Family changing room has level access shower with seat and grab rails. There is also a toilet and wash basin with grab rails. All wheelchair accessible

There is level access to all other showers, toilets and other facilities within the building.

There is a mother and baby room with fixed height surfaces for baby changing

Fully equipped laundry room with some space restrictions

Wash up accessible with wheelchair

TV room accessible with a wheelchair

Chemical toilet disposal building, accessible with wheelchair

Staff always on site for assistance

Nearby facilities:

Chainbridge Pub 300yds
Alice Springs golf course 400yds
Black Bear Pub and restaurant 1 mile
Big Pit Mining museum, Blaenavon
Fishing available nearby
Pony trekking at Abergavenny

Roman Fortress and baths at Caerleon
Raglan, Skenfrith and Abergavenny castles
Windsurfing, sailing and trout fishing at Llandegfedd Reservoir
Access to the Usk Valley Walk nearby
Millennium Stadium, Cardiff within 40 minutes
Leisure centres in Abergavenny, Monmouth, Pontypool and Newport
Monmouthshire& Brecon Canal within 10 minutes
Canoeing and rock climbing at Symonds Yat
Local market at Abergavenny on Tuesday and Friday

Rates: On application

Directions: Leave the M4 at junction 24. Travel north on to the A449. Turn off at the Usk Junction and in to Usk. Or from the M5/M50/A40 head south on the A449 to the Usk junction and into Usk

In the centre of Usk turn right for Abergavenny on the B4598. Travel about 4 miles, cross Chainbridge, travel a further 300 yards and the Caravan Park is on the right directly off the main road.

From Abergavenny follow the A40 on the roundabout and go under the railway bridge. Following the one way system signposted for Monmouth you must turn left for Usk on the B4598 before joining the A40 dual carriageway. After 4 miles turn right for Usk at the Charthouse Pub, travel a further two and a half miles and the Caravan Park is on the left 300yds before Chainbridge.

Nearest town/resort: Usk

Out and about: The historic town of Usk is only a short distance away. It has a very interesting museum that is well worth a visit. Head south to Caerleon and visit the Roman remains - the amphitheatre - the barracks - the baths - and the Roman Legionary Museum. More Roman remains, this time impressive well preserved walls and the foundations of buildings, can be seen at Caerwent, to the east of Caerleon. Newport is also well worth visiting. Here you can cross the River Usk on one of the only two transporter bridges in Britain. Dating from 1430, Raglan Castle and its Great Yellow Tower of Gwent are certainly worth a visit. Llandegfedd reservoir between Usk and Pontypool can be fished, and there is also good fishing on the River Usk. You can play a round of golf at the nearby Alice Springs Golf Club. At Blaenavon you can take a trip down Big Pit, now a coal mining museum, or visit the old iron works with its preserved workers cottages.

The pub, A to B: Turn left out of the Park, bearing to your left and crossing the Chainbridge over the River Usk. Take the sharp left turning just after the bridge and enjoy the leisurely one mile - twenty minute stroll up the lane to the hamlet of Bettws Newydd. The 16th century ***Black Bear Inn*** is at the crossroads in the village. It's well worth the walk in order to sample the selection of fine cask ales.

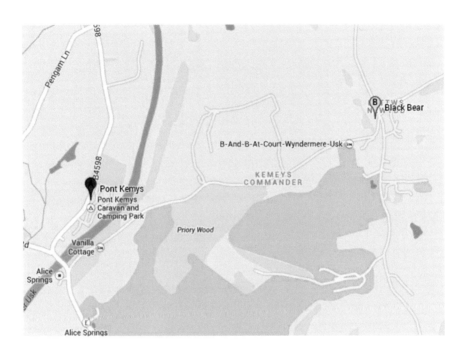

A. Pont Kemys to B. the Black Bear Inn

H. CRICCIETH

Llwyn Bugeilydd Caravan and Camping Site
Prop. Mr R. Roberts
Criccieth
Gwynedd
LL52 0PN
Tel: 01766 522235 or Manager (Carol) 01766 523140
www.llwynbugeilydd.co.uk
Email: cazzyanne1@hotmail.com

Open: March to October

Pitches for: 42 Tourers/Motorhomes/Tents can be accommodated at Llwyn Bugeilydd, with 42 16amp Hook-ups.

Acreage: The level site covers 5½ acres set in 52 acres of farmland.

Access: Good

Site location: Llwyn Bugeilydd is a pleasant camp site catering for Caravans, Tents ... or bring your Motorhome. Just along the B4411 it's the nearest camp site to Criccieth. The level site has a good wide tarmac entrance. It is sheltered to the north by the Mountains and Snowdonia National Park, with a view of Snowdon from the site. A very quiet pleasant site away from traffic noise. There is a regular bus service from the main gate. Gateway to the Lleyn Peninsular, Pwllheli, Abersoch and Aberdaron

Facilities: There's a modern shower block, with shaver and hairdryer points, separate sinks for clothes and cutlery all with plenty of free hot water -
16amp Electric Hook-ups
Toilets
Free Showers (one step up to toilets and showers)
Shaver and Dryer Points
Chemical Disposal Point
2 Stainless Steel Sinks
Close Cut Grass
Very Clean Facilities.

Dogs are welcome. There's a separate dog exercise field next to the site.

Nearby facilities: Llwyn Bugeilydd is the nearest camp site to Criccieth, near to the Golf Club, and within easy walking distance (one mile) to shops, sandy beaches, (safe for children) and the 13th century castle, open to the public. There are Local Food Shops, Pubs, Restaurants, Chinese Takeaway, Tennis Courts, Two Course Fisheries, Golf Course, Horse Riding, Sandy and Pebble Beaches all within a mile or so.

In nearby Porthmadog you will find the Ffestiniog and Welsh Highland Railways not to mention a wide variety of local shops including Tesco.

Not far away you will find Portmerion Italianate Village (where The Prisoner was filmed) and Castell Deudraeth.

Rates: On application

Directions: From the A55 take the A487 through Caernarfon, then just past Bryncir, turn right on to the B4411 and Llwyn Bugeilydd is on the left (3½ miles).

From Porthmadog travel along the A497 to Criccieth turning right in the centre along the B4411 Llwyn Bugeilydd is on the right (1 mile).

Nearest town/resort: Criccieth

Out and about: The ideal location for touring the Lleyn peninsula, from Criccieth in the south-east, down to Aberdaron at the western tip, and back to Llandwrog in the north-east. The attractions of the coastline are too numerous to mention but are a joy to behold - coves, bays, beaches, and superb cliff scenery abound. Tre'r Ceiri is the best preserved iron-age hill-fort in north Wales and stands at 1591 feet on the east peak of Yr Eifl. Inside its walls are numerous circular and rectangular huts covering an area of some 5 acres. The site was later occupied by the Romans who probably abandoned it circa 400 AD. Pwllheli is the unofficial capital of Lleyn and it is a mixture of seaside resort and market town. Aberdaron was the embarkation point for pilgrims crossing over to Ynys Enlli (Bardsey Island), which is also known as the island of 20,000 saints, and it is apparent that many pilgrims and holy men ended their days here. Access to the island is limited to bona-fide ornithologists and local people with permits.

The pub, A to B: Turning to your left on leaving the Campsite, walk the one mile down the hill into Criccieth and the junction with Stryd Fawr. Cross over the road and turn to your left down Stryd Fawr. You will find the Prince of Wales just down on the right. When you come out of the Prince of Wales, turn to your left and head straight up Stryd Fawr to the Bryn Hir Arms on the left. When you come out of the Bryn Hir Arms, turn to your left and continue on up Stryd Fawr, then turn left down Parciau Terrace to *The Castle Inn* with its cosy décor and great guest ales!

A. Llwyn Bugeilydd to B. The Castle Inn

I. CRICKHOWELL

Riverside Caravan & Camping Park
New Road
Crickhowell
Powys
NP8 1AY
Tel: 01873 810397
www.riversidecaravanscrickhowell.co.uk

Open: 1st March to 31st October

Pitches for: The very well-tended Park has 65 level touring pitches for tent, touring caravans and motor caravans.

Acreage: The 3½ acres park is set in delightful countryside on the edge of Crickhowell close to the River Usk.

Access: Good

Site location: A quiet, sheltered, level, grassy site surrounded by wonderful views. The adjacent riverside park is an excellent facility for all, including dog-walkers. Crickhowell town centre, 5 minutes' walk away, has numerous specialist shops including a first class delicatessen. Within a few minutes' walk from the park are several friendly pubs with good restaurants. A relaxing base from which to explore the surrounding area with the grand 17th century bridge, with 13 arches visible from the east end and only 12 from the west. You cannot fail to enjoy this thriving market town's charming country pubs. Riverside Caravan Park is snuggled between the Black Mountains and the Brecon Beacons, close to the Monmouthshire Brecon canal - a must for walking and cycling. And there are many walks around Crickhowell and the surrounding countryside.

Facilities: Riverside's excellent on-site facilities include:

Showers
Toilets
Laundry Room
10amp. Electricity Supply
Ice Pack Facility
Hard Standings
Chemical Toilet Disposal
Adults Only Site
No hang-gliders or paragliders
No single-sex groups.

Dogs are welcome but must be kept on a lead at all times and excercised in the adjacent riverside field

Nearby facilities: Golf, horse riding, fishing.

There are many walks around Crickhowell and the surrounding countryside, ranging from a circular town walk which takes about 45minutes, to other walks to suit all ages and the experienced. Leaflets are available in town in many of the shops including Crickhowell Adventure Gear which caters for outdoor activities including walking. Crickhowell is within easy reach of Table Mountain and the Brecon Beacons.

What's on in the area:
Royal Welsh Show
Brecon Jazz
Hay Festival
Abergavenny Food Festival
Monmouth Show

Places to visit:
Tretower Court and Castle
Brecon Mountain Railway
Big Pit National Mining Museum of Wales
Dan yr Ogof National Showcaves of Wales
Llangorse Activity Centre
Golden Castle Riding Stables
Black Mountain Chocolate
Dragonfly Cruises Brecon Canal
Brecon Beacons National Park
Museum of Life St. Fagans

Rates: On application

Directions: In Crickhowell, on the right, 500 yards along the A4077 from its junction with the A40.

Nearest town/resort: Crickhowell

Out and about: An ideal location for touring the Black Mountains and Brecon Beacons. This is excellent walking country. Abergavenny, just 5 miles to the east, is famous for its markets, while another old market town, Brecon, is only 14 miles to the west. There are numerous sites of historic interest close by including Llanthony Priory, Tretower Court and Castle, Raglan Castle, and the 'three castles' of Grosmont, Skenfrith and White Castle. The Brecon and Monmouthshire Canal meanders quietly along but a stone's throw away. For the book lover, Hay-on-Wye, the small border town famous for its bookshops, is a real treat. Go there via Talgarth and the A40 - A479 - A4078 - A438 and B4350. Return on the narrow unclassified mountain road through the Gospel Pass and the Vale of Ewyas, stopping at Wales' smallest chapel at Capel y Ffin, and at Llanthony Priory. Then follow the B4423 to Llanvihangel Crucorney and Wales' 'oldest inn' - The Skirrid Mountain Inn. Finally, along the A465 to Abergavenny and the A40 back to Crickhowell.

The pub, A to B: There's an excellent selection of hotels and pubs in and around Crickhowell. If you turn left out of the Park onto New Road and walk the 300 yards up to the town centre, taking the short-cut to the right 75 yards along up Lamb Lane and Bridge Street to High Street, you have the choice of three. As you walk up High

Street, The Britannia Inn is on your left and the Corn Exchange diagonally across the road on your right. The Bear Hotel is facing you across the square. If you're looking for more of a 'village' pub, turn right out of the campsite and walk the ¼ mile over the bridge and on through the fields to Llangattock and the Horse Shoe Inn on Beaufort Road. And if you're not really up to walking far, *The Bridge End Inn* is exactly where you would expect it to be – at the Crickhowell end of the bridge in Bridge Street. You are sure of a warm welcome and a good pint of ale here!

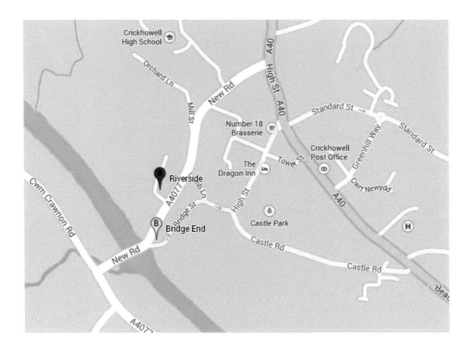

A. Riverside to B. The Bridge End Inn

J. DOLGELLAU

Tan y Fron Holiday Static & Touring Caravan and Camping Park
Arran Road
Dolgellau
Gwynedd
LL40 2AA
Tel: 01341 422638
www.campsitesnowdonia.co.uk
Email: info@tan-y-fron.co.uk

Open: All year for touring caravans/motor-homes/camper vans and camping near Dolgellau. Open 10 months of the year for static holiday homes.

Pitches for: Tan y Fron's 30, level, grassed camping pitches are terraced, with dedicated parking. Some pitches are available with electric hook-up. Its small Holiday Home Park of only 24 owner-occupied pitches is ideal for people who enjoy the relaxing atmosphere of a natural environment.

Acreage: This beautifully maintained and landscaped 3¼ acre caravan and camping holiday park is set in private grounds with an abundance of mature, landscaped gardens.

Access: Good

Site location: A quiet family owned and run park, open all year. The Park is the nearest campsite to the old market town of Dolgellau being only ½ mile away allowing you to leave your car and walk to sample a varied choice of nearby restaurants, pubs and shops. With Cader Idris as a background, tent pitches have scenic countryside views overlooking Dolgellau to the hills beyond. An ideal base for exploring Snowdonia National Park, Dolgellau, Gwynedd, the Mawddach Estuary…with the Coed y Brenin Forestry Centre and mountain biking 'Mecca' nearby.

Facilities:

Reception area:
A full range of leaflets, helpful hints and advice, menus of local places to eat, bus/train timetables etc. are available.
There is a small shop area with basic essentials.
Bottled and camping gas is available here for sale.
Ice packs can be frozen.
Wi-Fi Internet access (bring your own laptop).
Friendly staff always on hand to assist you.

Camping pitches:
Level camping pitches with scenic views.
Electric hook-up points.
Designated private parking.

Touring pitches:
Hard standing for caravan and car.
Grassed area.
Electric hook-ups.
Water hook-up.
Waste-water hook-up.
Good mobile phone and TV reception.
Some grassed pitches available.

Toilet and shower block:
Modern, centrally-heated Ladies and Gent's toilet blocks.
Shower cubicles with foldable seats, toilet cubicles, urinals and sinks in the Gent's.
Shower cubicles, toilet cubicles and sinks in the Ladies.
Both also have soap dispensers, mirrors, hand dryers and bins, coin operated hairdryers and coin operated electric socket.
Cleaned regularly and kept to a high standard.

Chemical toilet disposal point with tap.

Dish washing room with free hot water, sinks and surfaces.

Launderette:
This is equipped with:
One coin operated washing machine and two coin operated tumble dryers.
An ironing board attached to the wall with a metered iron.
A metered socket that can be used for any of your portable appliances.
A sink unit for hand washing clothes with metered hot water.
Open all day.

Security barrier:
This ensures that only those who should be on the Park are on the Park!

Dogs are not allowed.

Nearby facilities:

Beaches:
Barmouth
Fairbourne
Aberdyfi
Harlech
Portmeirion
Shell Island
Blackrock Sands

Walking:
This great site lists the best *walks near Dolgellau*, including the estuary, Cader Idris, the Precipice Walk and many others:
www.walking.visitwales.com, or follow the link on the Tan y Fron website *Things To Do Page* for more information.

The Mawddach Trail in particular is a well surfaced track on an old railway line from Dolgellau to Barmouth on the southern side of the estuary – easy for cycles, trailers, wheelchairs and feet.
Visit: www.mawddachtrail.co.uk, or follow the link on the Tan y Fron website *Thinks to Do Page* for more information.

The Mawddach Way is a three day 50km circular footpath walk right around the Mawddach Estuary.
Visit: www.mawddachway.co.uk, or follow the link on the Tan y Fron website *Things To Do Page* for more informatiom.

For information on **walks in Snowdonia,** visit the Snowdonia National Park website: www.eryri-npa.gov.uk, or follow the link on the Tan y Fron website *Things To Do Page* for information.

Panorama Walk, Barmouth's most famous walk. There is a car park and toilet at the top of the Panorama Road. Great views over the estuary.
Visit: www.mawddachway.co.uk, or follow the link on the Tan y Fron website *Things To Do Page.*

Fun stuff:
Crab lining from Barmouth Harbour
The Blue Lake – a flooded Slate Quarry
Talyllyn Railway
King Arthur's Labyrinth and Corris Craft Centre
The Centre for Alternative Technology
Go Ape – High Wire Forest Adventure
Dolgellau and Discover Dolgellau

Pony trekking:
Bwlchgwyn Farm Pony Trekking Centre

Sailing:
Merioneth Yacht Club
Dovey Yacht Club
Bala Sailing Club

Golf:
Dolgellau Golf Club
Aberdovey Golf Club
Royal St. Davids Golf Course in Harlech

Biking:
Bike hire and repairs – Dolgellau Cycles.
Snowbikers for details of the area's way marked trails. You can even hire mountain bike guides.
Tan y Fron is on the National Cycle Network Route-8 which you can follow in a figure of 8 around the Mawddach Estuary – it takes around 8 hours and 80km.
Mountain Biking Wales for more trails.

The Mawddach Trail is the nearest trail.
Coed y Brenin is the best known with tracks for all levels of skill.
The circuit of Cader Idris is not to be missed.

Adventure and water sports:
Outdoor Adventure Activities, Llanbedr (16 miles)
Up4adventures, Dolgellau
Balawatersports (20 miles)
National Whitewater Rafting Centre (20 miles)
Geocaching
Kitesurfing

Castles:
Visit Cadw for many of the old sites: cadw.wales.gov.uk
Harlech
Criccieth
Castell y Bere built by the Welsh Prince Llywelyn the Great in the 13th century
Cymer Abbey – ruins of a Cistercian abbey founded in 1198
St. Celynin's – Llangelynin medieval church

Local history:
Bronze Bell Shipwreck Exhibition, Ty Gwyn Museum (above Davy Jones' Locker),
The Quay, Barmouth. Tells the story of the nearby wreck of 1709, and of the salvage
operation.
Quaker Trail Dolgellau.
Llanfair Slate Caverns (18 miles).
Corris Mine Explorers (15 miles).

Fishing:
Lynn Jericho
Dolgellau Angling Association
Sea fishing trips run from Barmoutyh Harbour
Talyllyn Lake

Bird watching and nature:
There are two within easy walking distance:
Coed Garth Gell RSPB nature reserve and
Arthog Bog RSPB nature reserve.
Bird Rock or Craig yr Aderyn – of European importance as a traditional breeding and
roosting site.
Coed Ganllwyd Nature Reserve.

Pubs and eating:
Bwyty Dylanwad Da Restaurant, Bar, Wine Shop.
The Meirionydd hotel/restaurant.
T H Coffee Shop, Parliament House, Heol Glyndwr, Dolgellau, Gwynedd, LL40 1BB,
Tel: 01341 423552 - marvellous café with broadband, games, great food.
Y Sospan, Queen's Square, Dolgellau, Gwynedd, LL40 1AR, Tel: 01341 423174 -
lovely intimate Welsh restaurant.
George 111 – a historic pub on the estuary by the wooden toll bridge.

Bwyty Mawddach.
Bistro Bermo.

Entertainment:
Discover Dolgellau
Dolgellau Music Club
Ty Siamas folk centre
Barmouth Nightlife
Visit Mid Wales What's on
Dragon Theatre, Barmouth
Theatr Harlech

Steam trains:
Fairbourne Narrow Gauge Railway
Welsh Highland Railway
Corris Railway

Rates: On application

Directions: On the eastern access road into the centre of Dolgellau from the A470 junction near the junction with the A494.

Nearest town/resort: Dolgellau

Out and about: Dolgellau is situated in a wide and fertile valley on the River Wnion under the northern slopes of Cader Idris. Owain Glyndwr assembled the last Welsh parliament here in 1404. Gold was mined in the nearby Gwynfynydd mine until 1935 – the Queen's wedding ring is made from Dolgellau gold. Just 10 miles to the west is the delightful seaside town of Barmouth on the estuary of the river Mawddach. If you are a hill walker then to climb to the summit of Cader Idris (2927 feet) will prove to be an invigorating experience! Follow the A470 in an easterly direction and you pass through Bwlch Oerddrws – believed to be the site of the battle of Camlan where King Arthur was mortally wounded. On through Mallwyd and join the A489 at Cemmaes Road and arrive at Machynlleth with its remarkable clock tower. Here also is Owain Glyndwr's parliament building. Turn right at the clock tower and return along the A487 to rejoin the A470 at Cross Foxes and return to Dolgellau. A round trip of some 40 miles but well worth it, as the scenery is absolutely stunning! Visit lonely Castell y Bere, a short distance to the north of Abergynolwyn; and Llanfihangel y Pennant close by. Here is the ruined cottage where Mary Jones lived as a child. She is remembered for her epic walk barefoot across the mountains to purchase a bible from Thomas Charles in Bala. The lovely Talyllyn narrow gauge railway runs from Abergynolwyn to Towyn on the coast.

The pub, A to B: On turning left out of the Park, at the end of the gentle 600 yards stroll down Arran Road into Dolgellau, you will be rewarded with a selection of pubs from which to choose. After crossing over the bridge and bearing left, you will see on your left, tucked away in Smithfield Square, the ***Unicorn Inn*** - a warm and friendly pub. On leaving the Unicorn, turn left and follow the one-way system round through Eldon Square into Llys Owain/Queen's Square, where you will find the Royal Ship Hotel in front of you. On Leaving the Royal Ship, turn left and continue on following the one-way system into Bridge Street where you will find The Stag Inn on your left. On leaving The Stag, turn to your right and retrace your footsteps back along Bridge Street, taking the left hand turn just before you reach the Royal Ship, and into Mill Street where you will find the Kross Keys a little way along on your left.

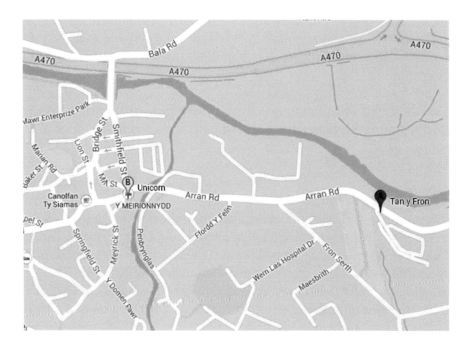

A. Tan y Fron to B. the Unicorn Inn

K. LAUGHARNE

Antshill Caravan Park
Laugharne
Carmarthenshire
SA33 4QN
Tel: 07977110095
www.antshill.co.uk
Email: Contact_Us@antshill.co.uk

Open: Easter to October

Pitches for: 60 level touring pitches cater for tents, motor homes and touring caravans; seasonal pitches are available. There are also pitches for static caravans.

Acreage: The Park consists of 8½ acres situated in the countryside of South West Wales with peaceful and pleasing rural views.

Access: Good

Site location: An elevated site ½ mile from Laugharne on the Taf Estuary, 5 miles from Pendine Sands. The campsite is within walking distance of the historic township of Laugharne, which is famous for Laugharne Castle and Welsh Poet Dylan Thomas who did much of his writing in the boat house. The Township holds events such as the Laugharne Festival, Carnival Week and a Regatta. Antshill is also only a short drive from scenic coast line and award winning beaches. Country walks, river and sea fishing, horse riding and many other activities are all close at hand.

Facilities: The touring and camping area offers spacious pitches with electric hook-up points. Additional facilities include: a newly built shower block with electric shaver points and hairdryers, family rooms, a launderette and dish wash rooms. All campers have full use of site facilities including the club house which provides live entertainment at weekends, bar meals and Sunday lunches. The site also has an outdoor heated swimming pool, a children's play area and a games room.

Club House:
Fully licenced bar
Sky TV
Bar snacks
Sunday lunch
Live entertainment (high season only)
Kids games room
Bingo

Swimming Pool:
Heated outdoor swimming pool (high season only)

Kids Play Area:
Climbing frame
Swings

Slides

New Toilet Shower Block:
Brand new facilities
Free heated showers

Dogs are not allowed

Nearby facilities:

Laugharne:
Laugharne Town:
A picturesque coastal town in South West Wales famous having been the home of Dylan Thomas.
Dylan Thomas Boathouse:
Dylan Thomas with his wife Caitlin and three children lived in the Boathouse from 1949 to 1953.
Laugharne Castle:
Over 20 years the castle has undergone painstaking archaeological investigation and restoration.
St Martin's Church:
The location of Dylan Thomas' grave.
Laugharne Pottery:
Laugharne Pottery has been producing fine designs in traditional handcrafted stoneware since 1971.
Laugharne Glass Studio:
World renowned originators of fine glass designs in hallmarked Silver Overlay.
Hill's Farm Stables:
Horse riding and pony trekking, along Pendine beach, in both Carmarthenshire and Pembrokeshire's idyllic countryside.
Cors garden:
An extraordinary, exotic garden in the grounds of an excellent restaurant.

Popular Attractions:
Oakwood:
Theme Park.
Go Ape:
Tree top adventure with ropes, ladders and zip wire.
Pembrey Dry Ski Slope:
Pembrey has great ski and snowboard rental facilities.
Folly Farm:
Adventure Park and Farm.
Manor House Wildlife Park:
As seen on BBC One.
Botanical Garden of Wales
Pembrey Country Park:
202 hectares of beautiful parkland, beaches and family attractions overlooking Carmarthen Bay.
Gwili Steam Railway:
A volunteer run steam railway using standard gauge track.

Pemberton's Welsh Chocolate Farm:
Smell, taste, see, drink, touch, listen to and absorb all the flavours of fine award winning chocolate.

Merlin Hill Centre:
Merlin, guardian to King Arthur is said to have lived and died in a cave on Merlin's Hill.

Morfa Bay Outdoor Centre:
Outdoor activities which include abseiling/rock climbing, coasteering, sea kayaking, land Yachting and many more…

Battlefield Live:
Outdoor combat team game using infra red gaming guns.

Shaggy Sheep Wales:
Outdoor activities which include 4x4 Driving, Gorge Scrambling, Canyoning White Water Rafting, Horse Riding, Quad Biking, Hovercrafting and many more...

Carmarthen Golf Club:
An 18 hole, par 71 course with magnificent views of the surrounding countryside.

Beaches:
Amroth Beach:
Amroth is a wide south facing sandy beach with 'Blue Flag' status and Seaside Award.

Pendine Sands:
A seven mile long beach, a mixture of sand, shells and rocks on the shores of Carmarthen Bay.

Wiseman's Bridge:
A large sandy beach with a few pebbles facing south east. Access via a slip way. Café and free car park.

Saundersfoot:
This is a sandy beach with a small harbour. It has walks which are part of the Pembrokeshire Country National Park coast walk.

Tenby:
Tenby maintains a high standard for it's beaches, offering plenty of facilities and boasting various environmental awards.

Historic:
St Peter's Church, Carmarthen:
The church's recorded history dates from 1100 when it was conferred by Henry 1 on Battle Abbey.

Carmarthen Castle:
The castle on its rocky eminence must have dominated the medieval town of Carmarthen.

Carmarthenshire Museum:
The museum presents many aspects of Carmarthenshire's rich and varied past.

Llansteffan Church:
Founded by Sant Ystyffan (Saint Stephen) in the 6th C.

Llansteffan Castle:
The castle stands on top of a hill with the sea and shore stretching out beneath.

Kidwelly Castle:
Founded in 1106 the stone structure dates from the 13th C.

Colby Woodland Garden:

A glorious informal garden with year round scents and colours. Shop, tea room and gallery.

Click on the links on the Antshill website *Local Attractions Page* for more information on these attractions.

Rates: On application

Directions: From junction of A40, A477 and A4066 at St. Clears, travel south on A4066 for 3½ miles and turn east as signed. The campsite is only ½ mile from Laugharne.

Nearest town/resort: Laugharne

Out and about: The small town of Laugharne is probably best known as having been the home of the world famous poet Dylan Thomas. No visit to Laugharne is complete without seeing The Boathouse, where Dylan and his wife Caitlin lived. A short distance from The Boathouse is the shed overlooking the estuary from where Dylan did much of his writing. A simple cross in Laugharne churchyard marks Dylan and Caitlin's grave. The 12th century castle is in the town itself and is also worthy of a visit. Five miles to the west of Laugharne are Pendine Sands where Malcolm Campbell set a world land speed record. The ancient market town of Carmarthen is just 13 miles to the north east of Laugharne and the National Botanic Garden of Wales is only another 8 miles further east at Llanarthne.

The pub, A to B: A gentle downhill stroll of ½ mile after turning left out of the Campsite will bring you into Laugharne with its selection of hostelries. Keep a look out for *Browns Hotel* on your left on King Street as you make your way in. Much frequented by Dylan Thomas, it's an excellent place to relax and enjoy your end of the day pint! A little way along on the same side as Browns, only now in Market Street, you will come across The New Three Mariners. About 150 yards further along from The Three Mariners on the other side of the road is Grist Square. Here you will both The Cross House and The Fountain Inn.

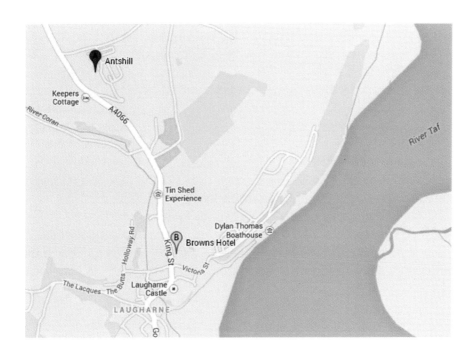

A. Antshill to B. Browns Hotel

L. LLANDOVERY

Erwlon Caravan & Camping Park
Brecon Road
Llandovery,
Carmarthenshire
SA20 0RD
Tel: 01550 721021/720332
Fax: 01550 721021
www.erwlon.co.uk
Email: peter@erwlon.uk

Open: All year

Pitches for: Erwlon is a spacious site with 75 level touring pitches for caravans, tents and motor-caravans; with super-pitches and plenty of landscaped pitches available.

Acreage: The family run Park covers 5 acres and is a part of Erwlon Farm,

Access: Good

Site location: Alongside the River Gwydderig, Erwlon is within easy walking distance of the ancient borough town of Llandovery, only ½ mile east of the town off the A40 towards Brecon. With a warm welcome, all level touring pitches and excellent award winning facilities, it is an ideal base for touring, walking or cycling in South West Wales. You can get to all the primary attractions and coastal resorts of South West Wales within a comfortable drive of about 1 to 1½ hours and there are a number of circular tours you can follow to take in the beautiful countryside on your way.

Facilities: There are facilities available to meet just about your every need.

The award winning amenity block is kept to the highest standard of cleanliness

The family rooms are very popular with young families but are also great for those that need a little assistance or just need that extra space. Every Family Room has a hair and hand dryer while one room is fitted to meet the needs of disabled visitors and one room is fitted with a baby changing table. They are all free and you don't need keys, codes etc. for access.

Fully serviced super-pitches include a hard standing, your own water point and grey waste discharge plus electric hook-up. If you want to put up an awning don't forget to take suitable pegs!

Wi-Fi broadband internet access is available across the Park; just take your lap-top. If you don't have a serviced pitch you can plug in at the Reception area.

Not only can you freeze your ice packs, you have the use of a fridge freezer to keep all your provisions fresh.

Erwlon is a natural, quiet retreat, so don't expect any club houses, shops etc. Llandovery is just down the road and you can take a stroll to the local cafes, pubs, shops etc.

Here is a list of facilities available at the Park:

BBQ Area
Battery Charging Point
Chemical Disposal
Children's Playground
Disabled Facilities
Dogs Welcome
Drain Hook-up
Electric Hook-up
Electric Shaver Point
Fishing
Fully Serviced
Gas Available
Hard Standing
Ice Pack Facility
Internet
Laundry Room
Other Pets Welcome
Rallies Welcome
Showers
Telephone
Toilet Block
Washing Up Facilities
Water Hook-up

Family Rooms include shower, WC & washbasin

Motorcaravan Service Point with black & grey waste discharge

Within easy walking distance of Llandovery, with pubs, cafes and supermarket

Dog are welcome

Erwlon's Access Statement is available for you to see on the Erwlon website *Information Page*

Nearby facilities:

Llandovery:
This appealing little market town stands at the confluence of the Rivers Bran, Gwennol and Tywi, so its Welsh name, Llanymddyfri (meaning 'the church amid three waters' is particularly apt. More information about the town and nearby villages can be found on the Erwlon website *Out and About Page.*

Castles and Ancient Heritage:

There are at least seven Castles in Carmarthenshire and within a maximum of forty minutes' drive from Erwlon. Add a few Abbeys, some Roman Sites and as many Churches and Chapels as you can cope with. Visit: www.cadw.wales.gov.uk or click on the link on the Erwlon website *Attractions Page* for more information.

Gardens:

Erwlon is located in a region rich in gorgeous green spaces, from man-made masterpieces like The National Botanic Garden of Wales or the restored splendour of Aberglasney to the spectacular natural beauty of the Cambrian Mountains or our National Parks along the Pembrokeshire Coast or over the Brecon Beacons.

The 'One Big Garden' website: www.onebiggarden.com is also a useful introduction to some of the premier, formal garden attractions of South West Wales.

Carmarthenshire Gardens:

With its verdant rolling landscapes and headlining horticultural attractions, it's no surprise that Carmarthenshire has become known as 'The Garden of Wales. From the ultra-modern National Botanic Garden of Wales in the Tywi Valley to Aberglasney with its beautiful 16th and 17th century garden to the fascinating Hywel Dda Centre, garden lovers will find something for them.

Pembrokeshire:

The abundance of natural flora, excellent garden attractions and spectacular landscapes combine to give Pembrokeshire a deserved reputation as a paradise for those who love the outdoor life. Almost a third of the county, including the entire coastal strip is in the Pembrokeshire National Park and there are gardens in natural settings to visit too.

Swansea Bay:

Swansea Bay includes the Gower Peninsular; the UK's first ever designated Area of Outstanding Natural Beauty and one of the country's finest wild areas. Swansea Bay itself is protected by hills and warmed by the sea, creating a micro-climate in which tender plants flourish. Ideal for all the wonderful gardens and parks for you to visit.

Click on the link on the Erwlon website *Attractions Page* for more information.

Leisure Parks:
Oakwood Theme Park, Canaston Bridge, Narberth

Museums:
Big Pit - National Coal Museum, Blaenavon

Outdoor and Adventure:
Click on the link on the *Erwlon Activities Page* for more information.

Activities:
Bird Watching
Cycling
Fishing
Mountain Boarding
Pony Riding
Click on the links on the Erwlon *Activities Page* for more information.

Day Trips:

Suggestions for tours to visit the sights and attractions all over South Wales from your base at Erwlon can be found on the Erwlon website *Day Trips Page.*

Rates: On Application

Directions: ½ mile east of Llandovery off the A40 towards Brecon.

Nearest town/resort: Llandovery

Out and about: Situated at the edge of the western part of the Brecon Beacons National Park the Campsite is an ideal base for walking the Carmarthen Fans. St. Mary's church is the burial place of William Williams Pantycelyn, one of Wales' most prolific hymn writers, whose home was at Pantycelyn farmhouse some three miles away at Pentretygwyn. Near the village of Trapp are the ruins of Carreg Cennen Castle perched high on its rugged crag. Just the other side of Llandeilo, to the south-west, are the ruins of Dinefwr Castle, Dryslwyn Castle and and the 19th century folly Paxton's Tower. Llyn Brianne to the north of Llandovery is well worth visiting, as are the Roman gold mines at Pumsaint to the northwest. In Llandovery itself, there is a visitor centre combining a museum, which is full of interest.

The Pub, A to B: Llandovery is well blessed with hotels and public houses, as you will soon discover when you stroll the ½ mile from the Park into the town. Turn to your left as you leave by the rear entrance in the far corner of the Park and follow the A40 into town. First on your right is The Kings Arms on High Street. Crossing over the road, a little further along High Street is *The Bluebell,* or Y Gloch Las. This is a friendly pub welcoming locals and visitors alike where you can relax and enjoy a good pint of real ale. Next along on the left is *The White Hall Hotel,* which is at the start, and not the end, of High Street. If you venture across the road from the White Hall in the direction of Stone Street you will see *The Kings Head Inn* on your left (and is actually in Market Street). Making your way up Stone Street you will find The Greyhound Inn on the right and the Plough Hotel on the left, both about half way up the street. Making a U turn and walking back down Stone Street, turning right at the Kings Head, into Market Square, you can seek out The Red Lion. Continuing on along Market Square and turning off to your left you will come across The Bear Inn on the corner with King's Road. Turn to your right and *The Castle Hotel* is just along on the opposite side where the A40 is at its narrowest. Carry on along the A40/King's Road out of the town centre and continue to follow the A40 as it bends to the right along Queensway. It's about another 400 yards along Queensway to The North Western on the right hand side, and a further 400 yards after will bring you to your last port of call, The Lord Rhys, on your left hand side close to the railway station in College View. That's eleven in all!
If you consider the full itinerary to be just a little too much for one evening why not concentrate on a number of the hostelries in and around the heart of the town, namely *The Bluebell, The White Hall, The Kings Head* and *The Castle.*

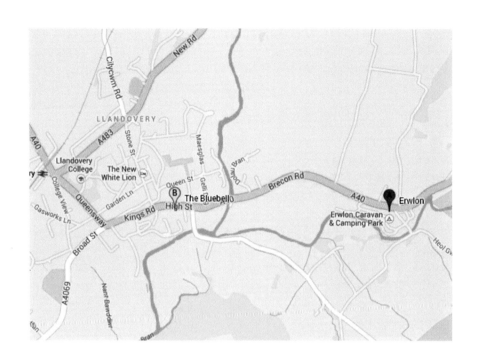

A. Erwlon to B. The Bluebell/Y Gloch Las

M. LLANGORSE

Lakeside Caravan and Camping Park
Llangorse Lake
Brecon
Powys
LD3 7TR
Tel: 01874 658226
www.llangorselake.co.uk
Email: holidays@llangorselake.co.uk

Open: 3rd week of March to 1st November

Pitches for: Lakeside Caravan and Camp Site has 40 pitches for tents, touring caravans and motor homes. Some hard standing pitches for touring caravans and motor homes with electric hook-up points. Grass pitches are also available for tents with or without electric hook-up points; these can also be used for touring caravans and motor homes.
In addition to the Caravan and Camp Site, Static Caravan Hire is also available, with both 4 berth and 6 berth caravans for hire. These holiday homes are fully equipped with a shower, toilet, gas cooker, microwave, fire etc.

Acreage: The Park occupies 14 acres of land very close to Llangorse Lake.

Access: Good

Site location: A level site situated close to Llangorse Lake, the largest natural lake in South Wales, in the heart of the Brecon Beacons National Park and Black Mountains. The Park is adjacent to Llangorse Common which leads down to the lake in an area teeming with wildlife. Surrounded by the stunning scenery of the Brecon Beacons, the Caravan and Camp Site offers many opportunities for those interested in outdoor activities.

Facilities: Lakeside Caravan and Camping Park is privately owned and managed and your welcome is warm.

The Caravan and Camp Site offers toilet and shower blocks (showers 20p), a chemical disposal point, laundry, washing up area and a children's play area.

There are some hard standing pitches for touring caravans and motor homes with electric hook-up points. Grass pitches are also available for tents with or without electric hook-up points; these can also be used for touring caravans and motor homes.

The Shop and Reception at Lakeside Caravan & Camping Park stocks various food supplies, souvenirs, camping and Calor gas, plus additional camping and watercraft goods.

Next to the Shop is Lakeside Restaurant, which provides hot meals and snacks.

Lakeside Bar & Beer Garden offers entertainment most weekends in high season.

Pool tables, TV available in the Bar (open weekends and all week during main holidays). The Beer Garden is a superb place to sit, have a drink and enjoy the views of the Brecon Beacons.

Caravan Hire is available at Lakeside. For details visit the Lakeside Caravan and Camping Park website *Caravan Hire Page.*

Lakeside Boat Hire can arrange rowing/fishing boats, canoes/kayaks, pedaloes and sailing dinghies. You can also launch your own craft from their slipway, be it for water-skiing, sailing, fishing or just to pass a few hours on the lake.

Llangorse Lake is renowned for its Pike Fishing and water skiing is also allowed on the lake. Visit the Lakeside Caravan and Camping Park website *Lake Page* for details.

Dogs are welcome. A maximum of two well-behaved pets per booking are allowed on the site, but must be kept on leads. They must not be left unattended at any time. Pets should be exercised off the site but owners are responsible for cleaning up any mess their animals make. Dogs must be kept on a lead at all times when on the site.

Nearby facilities: Llangorse village offers pony trekking, an indoor climbing centre and two local pubs (Recommended Local Pubs for meals can be found on the Lakeside Caravan and Camping Park website *Links Page*).

There is a huge choice of footpaths and bike trails within the Brecon Beacons National Park, or, from the Caravan and Camp Site you can follow the footpath around Llangorse Lake.

The Llangorse Crannog Centre, a thatched round house, containing historical and environmental information regarding the Crannog and Llangorse Lake is well worth a visit. The Crannog Centre, which is reached by a wooden walkway out into the waters of Llangorse Lake, gives you exceptional views of Pen y Fan the highest summit in the Breacon Beacons. An idyllic setting, the Crannog Centre is now available as a Wedding Venue.

Rates: On application

Directions: Llangorse can be approached from three directions:-

From the North you leave the A438 at Bronllys and head towards Talgarth. In Talgarth take the B4560 to Llangorse.

From the East (i.e. from Abergavenny), take the A40 towards Crickhowell and Brecon, carry on until you reach Bwlch village, turn right at the war memorial statue - sign posted Llangorse (B4560). Follow this road until you reach Llangorse village. In the village, drive past The Castle Inn on the right, then The Red Lion on your left, then take the first left after the Red Lion. After 100 metres take the next left turn which is signed 'Llyn/Lake'. Go over the cattle grid, carry straight on and Lakeside

Caravan Park shop and reception is 250 metres after the cattle grid on the left-hand side.

From the West leave the A40 at Bwlch taking the B4560 to Llangorse then follow the instructions as from the east.

Navigation Information:
Post Code LD3 7TR
OSX 3134 OSY 2273

Nearest town/resort: Brecon

Out and about: The site is situated on the shore of the largest natural lake in South Wales. You can enjoy all the on lake activities and venture into the surrounding countryside. Nearby Mynydd Troed (1997 feet) and Mynydd Llangorse (1661 feet) are excellent viewpoints and are both easily climbed. The historic town of Brecon is only 6 miles away. Here you can stroll along the banks of the river Usk, visit The South Wales Borderers Museum with its vast collection of memorabilia relating to the Zulu War and the battle of Rorke's Drift, or visit the Cathedral. For a gentle stroll you can pick up the Monmouthshire and Brecon Canal on the eastern edge of the town, or for a much more vigorous walk why not climb to the summit of Pen y Fan (2907 feet) in the nearby Brecon Beacons, the highest point in South Wales? The 'book town' of Hay-on-Wye is only thirteen miles away. A drive from Llangorse to Bwlch, turning right onto the A40, then within 1½ miles turning left into Talybont on Usk, through the village, then left over the canal, on past Talybont Reservoir, and on to Pontsticyll on the outskirts of Merthyr Tydfil, is truly rewarding. Being so near to Merthyr Tydfil it is well worth visiting the town which at one time was 'The Iron Capital of the World'. Here you can visit the museum housed in Cyfarthfa Castle, and the birthplace of Dr. Joseph Parry in Chapel Row. Joseph Parry was one of Wales' most prolific composers and one of his most famous works is 'Myfanwy' – 'the greatest love song ever written'.

The pub, A to B: Walking out of the Campsite and turning left across the common away from the lake, over the cattle grid and up the lane, then turning right, will bring you to Llangorse village. It's only about ½ mile so it's not too testing, and your reward will be awaiting you in the centre of the village. There are just the two pubs; The Red Lion on your right and just around the bend on your left is *The Castle Inn* - a very agreeable inn!

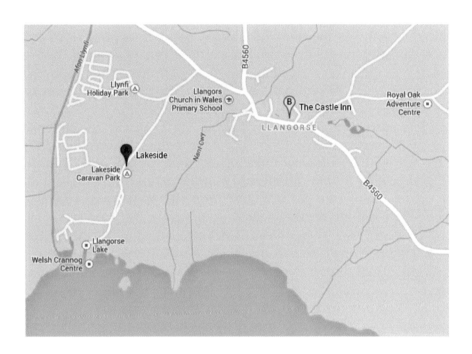

A. Lakeside to B. The Castle Inn

Bodnant Caravan Park

Proprietors Mrs. Ermin Kerry-Jenkins & Mr. Glyn Jenkins
Nebo Road
Llanrwst
Conwy Valley
LL26 0SD
Tel: 01492 640248
www.bodnant-caravan-park.co.uk
Email: ermin@bodnant-caravan-park.co.uk

Open: Beginning March to end October

Pitches for: All 35 caravan and motor-caravan pitches are multi-serviced pitches with 16 amp electric hook-up, TV hook-ups, water taps and grey waste disposal. Some hard-standing pitches are available.
All 14 tent pitches which are in a separate field have electric and TV hook-ups. Most tent pitches with the electric hook-ups are approx. 9x9 metres. ***Please note*** the site cannot accept tents larger than 5x6 metres including guide ropes.
The site is all level.
The pitches are either grass or hard-standing.
There is a separate field for caravan rallies.
There are 2 holiday caravans for hire.

Acreage: A small, quiet, pretty 4 acre farm site

Access: Good

Site location: Bodnant enjoys a picturesque location on the outskirts of the market town of Llanrwst in the beautiful Conwy Valley.
The Park has won the *'Wales in Bloom'* competition covering the whole of Wales, for touring caravans for 26 consecutive years with our many floral features and an array of old farm implements of a bygone era. Many customers return year after year to enjoy the gardens and relaxed, friendly atmosphere. The site is renowned even as far as Europe.
The site is all level, easily accessed, sheltered by trees and bordered by Nant y Goron stream, which runs into the River Conwy. The site is situated within 10 minutes walking distance from the town, opposite the Leisure Centre on the B5427 Nebo Road from Llanrwst, and is clearly signposted at the junction with the A470.

Facilities:

All 35 caravan and motor-caravan pitches are multi-serviced pitches with 16 amp electric hook-up, TV hook-ups, water taps and grey waste disposal.

Some hard-standing pitches are available.

Wi-Fi is available on the site (there is a charge for this).

All 14 tent pitches which are in a separate field have electric and TV hook-ups. Most tent pitches with the electric hook-ups are approx. 9x9 metres. *Please note* the site cannot accept tents larger than 5x6 metres including guide ropes.

There are two well- equipped holiday caravans for hire.

The toilet blocks have free hot water and showers. The larger toilet block is heated. There is also a block with disabled facilities.

A covered dishwashing area.
Chemical disposal point.
Recycling collection area.
Small playfield.
Dog walk.
Telephone box.

Access Statement: *Please click on the link on the Bodnant Caravan Park website Home Page to view the Park's access statement for information on access to the caravan and camping site for those with disabilities.*

The Park also has a small farm stocking sheep, hens, ducks, geese and guinea fowl. The site is well known for its animal cemetery, marked with little white crosses where children often leave posies of wildflowers.

Many varieties of birds can be found on the site; woodpeckers, goldcrests, mistle thrushes, redstarts, tree creepers, siskins, nuthatches, herons, buzzards, sparrow hawks and house martins are just a few apart from the more common garden species such as tits and blackbirds. When dusk falls the bats come out. The local Llanrwst agricultural show is held every August just a few fields away and the local sheepdog trials are held locally in July. The Owners' own sheepdogs can sometimes be seen herding their sheep, ducks (and customers who haven't paid!!)

Dogs are welcome. Dogs should be exercised on the dog-walk or off the site. They must be kept under control and must not be allowed to foul any part of the site. Dogs should not he left unattended in caravans/tents or cars especially in hot weather.

Nearby facilities: The Conwy Valley at the edge of Snowdonia is a place of unsurpassed beauty; clothed, it is said, in every shade of green imaginable. Despite the farming of its lands, the planting of great swathes of forest, building of roads and the railway, the valley has remained relatively unchanged throughout the centuries. Apart from the natural beauty of its rivers, lakes and vistas of the rugged Snowdonia Mountains there are numerous places of interest to visit during your stay.

Llanrwst: the 'capital' of the Conwy Valley is an ancient market town built on the banks of the River Conwy. The ancient three-arched stone bridge leads into a town made up of narrow streets offering a plethora of shops selling goods from everyday needs to home baked bread and Welsh delicacies to butchers shops selling locally produced lamb (some from Bodnant's own farm). There is something to suit all palates in the variety of restaurants, bistros, cafes, take-aways and olde worlde tea-rooms.

There is a wealth of culture and heritage in the Conwy Valley, including the following:

St. Crwst's Church, Llanrwst (½ mile):
15th century church with beautiful carved rood screen, effigy of Hywel Coetmor and stone coffin of Llywelyn the Great.

Almshouses, Llanrwst (½ mile):
recently restored 17th Century Almshouses.

Tu Hwnt i'r Bont, Llanrwst (½ mile):
Welsh afternoon teas are served in this ancient courthouse with its low oak beams, now in the keeping of the National Trust.

Gwydyr Castle, Llanrwst (1 mile):
16th century Manor House that was the ancestral home of the Wynns of Gwydyr.

Trefriw Wells Spa (3 miles):
This spa was said to have been discovered by soldiers from the XX Roman Legion.

Trefriw Woollen Mills (2 miles):
Working mill with large shop selling its products.

Crafnant & Geirionydd Lakes (4 miles):
Beautiful lakes nestling in the mountains above Trefriw.

Capel Garmon Cromlech (5 miles):
This burial chamber dates from circa 1800 BC.

Tree Top Adventure (3 miles):
Enjoy an action packed time on these aerial ropeways.

Betws-y-Coed (3 miles):
This most well-known of Welsh villages is in a picturesque location and offers many shopping opportunities.

Bodnant Garden, Eglwysbach (8 miles):
(after which Mrs. Kerry-Jenkins' mother named the caravan site - having been brought up on a farm adjacent to Bodnant Gardens).
Surely the greatest garden in Wales. Famous for its Laburn arch.

Further afield, but still within easy reach there are many more attractions to be discovered including:

Conwy Castle
Caernarfon Castle
Llechwedd Slate Caverns - Blaenau Ffestiniog

Slate Museum - Llanberis
Copper Mines - Llandudno & Beddgelert
Welsh Mountain Zoo - Colwyn Bay
Steam Railways - Ffestiniog Railway, Snowdon Mountain Railway and many others
Walking
Flora and Fauna
Pony trekking
Golf courses – Betws y Coed, Llandudno & Conwy
Beaches and Mountains.

The site is conveniently located for visiting the attractions of Snowdonia and North Wales.

Rates: On application

Directions: Turn off the A470 south in Llanrwst onto the B5427 signposted Nebo. The site is 300 yards on the right, opposite the Leisure Centre.
Grid Reference: 805 610.
Satnav: Use postcode LL26 0SD (O = zero).

Out and about: Situated in the Conwy Valley the site is an ideal location for touring North Wales. Travel down the valley for 12 miles to Conwy where you can visit Edward the First's impressive castle. Also take in Britain's smallest house on the quay. On the opposite side of the estuary is Llandudno, 'the Queen of the Welsh Resorts', with the sweep of its gracious and regal bay enclosed by The Great Orme and Little Orme. You can reach the summit of The Great Orme by cable railway or cabin lift where there are traces of very early human occupation. A short 4 mile journey south along the A470 will bring you to its junction with the A5 and the Waterloo Bridge. Make for Bettws y Coed and Swallow Falls. Also, visit The Ugly House just outside the village. Dolwyddelan Castle, a native Welsh castle, is another fine attraction worthy of a visit. Another place of interest is the Penygwryd Hotel, a solitary building in the place of the same name. Here was the headquarters for the successful Everest expedition of 1953, who did their preparatory training on the nearby peaks. It is a veritable museum of rock climbing, but a stone's throw from Wales' highest mountain Yr Wydda, or Snowdon (3660 feet).
Tucked away in the hills above Penmachno is Ty Mawr y Wibrnant, the birthplace of Bishop William Morgan who translated the bible into Welsh.

The pub, A to B: Turn left out of the Park and walk up Nebo Road to Llanrwst town which is only ¼ mile away. You will see the old bridge over the River Conwy on your left, and surprise, surprise, the *Pen y Bont* (which translates into English as the Bridgend) is on your right hand side in Ty'r Bont, or Bridge Street. A warm, cosy pub this…serving a good pint! Carrying along Ty'r Bont/Bridge Street into Ancaster Square you will see The Eagles Hotel on the left. Leaving the Eagles and continuing along your way you will see the Pen y Bryn Hotel just across the road on the right. A little further along you will come to Denbigh Street which goes off to your right. On turning right into Denbigh Street, The New Inn is on the left hand side at the very start of the street; with The Red Lion a little further down on the same side.

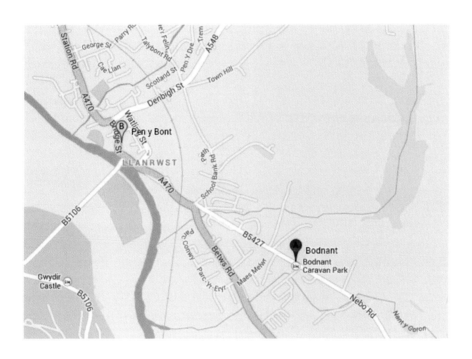

A. Bodnant to B. the Pen y Bont

O. LLANSANTFFRAID YM MECHAIN

Bryn Vyrnwy Holiday Park
Llansantffraid ym Mechain
Powys
SY22 6AY
Tel: 01691 828252
www.brynvyrnwyholidaypark.co.uk
Email: jan@brynvyrnwyholidaypark.co.uk

Open: 1st April (earlier if Easter falls prior to this date) to 31st October.

Pitches for: Bryn Vyrnwy Holiday Caravan Park has a small touring and camping area for tents, touring caravans and motor caravans. 40 level touring pitches are available on a level grassy area, with car parking and awning space next to the plots. 10 electric hook-up points are available (booking is recommended). Seasonal pitches for touring caravans, on hard standing grassy areas, are offered with electric hook up points.

Acreage: 3 acres. An ideal tranquil country setting and location nestling within 120 acres of farmland, there are four park areas, surrounded by rolling hills and stunning Welsh countryside

Access: Good

Site location: Bryn Vyrnwy Holiday Caravan Park, is situated mid-way between the medieval market town of Oswestry and the market town of Welshpool. A family owned and run, un-commercialised holiday park located just half a mile east of the village of Llansantffraid Ym Mechain in the heart of rural Mid Wales, yet just half a mile from the Shropshire/Powys border and the Welsh Marches. The market towns of both Oswestry and Welshpool are just 7 miles and Shrewsbury 20 miles.

Bryn Vyrnwy Holiday Caravan Park is maintained to a very high standard, with a large variety of flower and shrub borders, well cut and tended grass. Mature trees, traditional hedges, grassy banks and natural areas provide the ideal environment for wildlife, which can be seen in abundance. The free flowing river Vyrnwy, just a short walk from the park areas, nurtures many species of water life, offering both fast and slow running water with deep and shallow areas. Residents and visitors can enjoy a walk along the river bank, or partake in fishing on the ¾ mile river frontage.

Facilities: The Williams family have farmed at Bryn Vyrnwy for over 70 years. Doug, Jan and Edward take great pride in the presentation of the park and surrounding areas and offer a warm welcome and friendly service to visitors, holiday home owners, their families and friends.

Facilities at the park include:

Touring Caravans, Motor Homes and Camping Area:
Bryn Vyrnwy Holiday Caravan Park has a small touring and camping area. Pitches are available on a level grassy area, with car parking and awning space next to the

plots. 10 electric hook-up points are available (booking is recommended). A chemical disposal point is available and located by the toilet block. Convenient water points are available around the park.

Seasonal Pitches:
Seasonal pitches for touring caravans, on hard standing grassy areas, are offered with electric hook up points.

Caravan Storage:
Bryn Vyrnwy Holiday Caravan Park, has a specially designated, secure Touring Caravan and Motor Home storage area on hard standing. Storage is available all year round. Caravan washing facilities are also provided.

Toilet and Shower Block:
A small toilet and shower block is available, with separate ladies and gentlemen facilities. The wash basins are serviced with hot and cold water and the Showers facilities are token operated.

Launderette:
A small launderette is available within the park area offering a washing machine and tumble dryer.

Children's Play Area:
A small children's play area is provided, located away from the main caravan holiday parks, where children can play safely under the supervision of a responsible adult.

Fishing:
Fishing is available for Park residents to enjoy on our ¾ mile stretch of water on the River Vyrnwy.

Dogs are welcome. It is requested that dogs are kept on a lead on park areas but there are fields where they can have a good run. Management respectfully request that dog owners be responsible and clean up after their dogs at all times. If children take the family dog for a walk, again it is requested that they are able to control the dog(s) fully and that they be willing and able to clean up any mess.
Management reserve the right to exclude any dog that is out of control and/or showing signs of aggression.

Nearby facilities:

Places of interest within 1 hour:

Sightseeing:

Powis Castle & Garden (National Trust Property)
Nr. Welshpool. SY21 8RF:
The combination of terraces, formal and informal gardens make the garden at Powis a delight. The medieval Castle contains one of the finest collections of paintings and furniture in Wales.

Welshpool & Llanfair Light Railway:
Opened in 1903, this light gauge railway was created to link the Market Town of Welshpool and the rural community of Llanfair through the beautiful Mid-Wales countryside.

Powysland Museum & Canal Warf:
Montgomeryshire from the earliest prehistoric settlers to the 20th century population.

The Dingle Nurseries and Garden
Nr. Welshpool, SY21 9JD:
Derwen Garden Centre & Farm Shop.
Guilsfield, Nr Welshpool. SY21 9PH

Erddig (National Trust Property)
Nr. Wrexham, LL13 0YT:
One of the most fascinating houses in Britain, not least because of the close relationship between the family and their servants. The range of outbuildings includes stables, smithy, joiners' shop and saw mill. The large walled garden has been restored to its 18th century formal design.

Chirk Castle (National Trust Property)
Chirk, Nr. Wrexham, LL14 5AF:
Explore a magnificent medieval fortress of the Welsh Marches, complete with stark dungeons.

Chirk Aqueduct:
Constructed by Thomas Telford to carry the Llangollen Branch of the Shropshire Union Canal. Running alongside the aqueduct is the Chirk viaduct which was built to carry the Chester to Shrewsbury Railway line

Lake Vyrnwy & RSPB Reserve:
Set amid the remote and beautiful Berwyn Mountains, with spectacular waterfalls, and unspoilt countryside. Experience the walks and trails of the RSPB Reserve with viewpoints and hides around the lake to observe the amazing variety of birds, wildlife and scenery.

Pistyll Rhaeadr Waterfall:
Llanrhaeadr Ym Mochnant SY10 0BZ
One of the Seven Wonders of Wales. An enchanting waterfall nestling in the Berwyn Mountains, located above the village of Llanrhaeadr Ym Mochnant in the Tanat Valley. The highest waterfall in Wales at 240ft.

Towns & Cities:

Bala, Bala Lake & Bala Lake Railway:
A town with a wealth of history, located at the head of the famous Bala Lake.

Llangollen:
A small town steeped in myth and legend. Host to the Llangollen International Musical Eisteddfod in July. Attractions and activities include Plas Newydd, (formerly

home to the ladies of Llangollen), White water rafting on the river Dee, horse drawn boat trips along the beautiful Llangollen canal, Llangollen Railway and much more.

Oswestry:
Visit the vibrant medieval market town of Oswestry, steeped in local history and offers wide resources to our local Heritage. The Oswestry Heritage Centre, located in the old building of Oswestry's first school founded in 1407, close to St. Oswalds Parish Church offers a wealth of information and holds regular exhibitions of local arts and crafts. The town tourist centre can be found in the same building. Follow the Oswestry Town Trail leaflet, available from the Heritage Centre or the Tourist Information Centre at Mile End, to tour the towns many sites of historical interest. Wonder down narrow passageways which link streets with names that give an indication of the towns past history.

Welshpool:
Nestled in the upper reaches of the Severn Valley, the market town of Welshpool offers a wealth of history. Welshpool provides the opportunity to absorb the historical significance and the attractions of Borderlands and Welsh Marches.

Shrewsbury:
Medieval town oozing with history and historic buildings including Shrewsbury Castle and Shrewsbury Abbey. Home to the famous Shrewsbury Flower Show in August.

Wrexham:
Situated in the heart of the Welsh Border Lands, the town of Wrexham and surrounding areas are rich in history.

City of Chester:
The historic city of Chester was built by the Romans AD79. A city bursting with character and diversity. Explore the medieval rows and city walls. A wealth of shops and restaurants etc. Home to Chester Cathedral, Chester Zoo and Chester Race Course.

Further afield but under 2 hours:

The stunning West Wales coastline, hosting numerous seaside resorts from Aberystwyth up to Barmouth all easily accessible. Travel through Snowdonia National Park. Take a trip on numerous steam trains. Walk miles of rugged coastline. So much to see and do.

Activities:

The Flash Leisure Centre
Welshpool SY21 7DH

The Welsh Border Golf Complex
Nr. Welshpool SY2 8ER

Llanymynech Golf Club
Pant, Nr. Oswestry SY10 8LB

Oswestry Leisure Centre
Oswestry SY11 4QB

Welshpool Golf Club
Welshpool SY2 9AQ

Oswestry Golf Club
Oswestry SY11 4JJ

Rates: On application

Directions:

From Shrewsbury...follow the A5 for Oswestry...turn left onto the B4396 for Knockin...proceed through Knockin to Llynclys...at crossroads go straight over onto the A495 for Llansantffraid...approximately 2 miles turn left onto the A495 for Llansantffraid...approximately 2 miles Bryn Vyrnwy Holiday (Caravan) Park is located on your left.

From Wrexham...follow the A483 (A5) for Oswestry/Welshpool...continue on the A483 to Llynclys...at crossroads turn right onto the A495 for Llansantffraid...approximately 2 miles turn left onto the A495 for Llansantffraid...approximately 2 miles Bryn Vyrnwy Holiday (Caravan) Park is located on your left.

From Welshpool...follow the A483 for Oswestry...continue to Four Crosses...at the roundabout take the first exit onto the B4393 for Llansantffraid...approximately 3 miles enter the village of Llansantffraid over a single file river bridge...turn right at the junction onto the A495 sign posted Llanyblodwel/Oswestry...approximately ½ a mile Bryn Vyrnwy Holiday (Caravan) Park is located on your right

The reception is located at the Farm House, just 30 yards off the main road on your left as you enter into our large reception area, (formerly the farm yard).

Nearest town/resort: Oswestry/Welshpool

Out and bout: Ideally placed for visiting the Berwyn Mountains. Nearby Llanrhaeadr ym Mochnant is where Bishop William Morgan was incumbent when he translated the bible into Welsh. A narrow road leads from here to Pistyll Rhaeadr - Wales' highest waterfall - and higher than Niagra. Close by, Lake Vyrnwy, which has a visitor's centre, is the largest lake in Wales and is well worth a visit. Take a ride on the Welshpool and Llanfair Railway, which runs from Welshpool to Llanfair Caereinion. If you fancy a spot of shopping, nearby Welshpool is the place to go. While you are in Welshpool, be sure to visit stately Powis Castle, set in rich parkland of giant oaks just outside the town. Another place worth visiting is nearby Llanfyllin. An atmosphere of quiet always seems to pervade this lonely little place on the River Cain. Montgomery, once a county capital, is another small border town worthy of a visit. It is full of Tudor, Jacobean and Georgian houses, and Broad Street is one of the widest anywhere. The castle on the hilltop was erected during the reign of Henry the Third and replaced the original Norman motte-and-bailey castle that stood at the foot of the hill.

The pub, A to B: On turning left from the Campsite, a pleasant ½ mile stroll brings you to the village of Llansantffraid ym Mechain, which can be described as a half-mile-long street! There is a hostelry to be found at each end of the village. *The Sun Hotel* is the first for you to try. You will find it on the hand side of Waterloo Terrace just as you enter the village. It's a pleasant pub with a warm atmosphere – an ideal place to enjoy a pint. When you've done, you will need to walk the length of the village (500 yards) to The Lion Hotel, on the right hand side of Main Street, for your next pint!

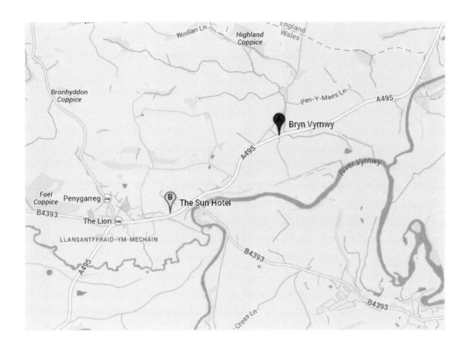

A. Bryn Vyrnwy to B. The Sun Hotel

Acorn Camping & Caravan Park

Ham Lane South,
Llantwit Major
Vale of Glamorgan
CF61 1RP
Tel: 01446 794024 (Office Hours: 9am – 8pm, 7 days a Week)
www.acorncamping.co.uk
Email: info@acorncamping.co.uk

Open: 1st February to 30th November

Pitches for: The Park has 105 pitches and can accommodate Touring Caravans, Motor Homes and Tents. The pitches are individually marked, some with trees and hedgerows providing extra privacy and shelter.

Acreage: The four and a half acre site is surrounded by farmland

Access: Good

Site location: Acorn Caravan & Camping Park is a small peaceful family owned rural site, situated on the Heritage Coast 1 mile from Llantwit Major and the beach. The four and a half acre site is surrounded by farmland. The whole site slopes gently towards the main entrance but is effectively quite level. Touring pitches have a mix of grass and hard standings, and space for one car parked next to the caravan. Tent pitches are grass and have parking for one car next to the tent. A family orientated site which operates a quiet time between 11pm and 7am. Excessive drinking and groups of young adults are not allowed.

Facilities: On site there is modern amenity building with free hot showers. Both the ladies and gents shower rooms also contain a separate hand basin and a place to get dressed away from the shower. There are free hairdryers in both the ladies and gents and shavers points in the gents.

The baby/family changing room contains a shower cubicle, toilet, and hand sink, along with potty, baby shower seat and baby changing board. The Park also has facilities for disabled guests, with a large open plan shower room. There is a dishwashing area and laundry area with two washing machines and a tumble dryer. There is also an iron and board, and an electric socket- perfect for those who can't live without their hair straighteners, which both run on electric tokens.

A range of camping gas and Calor gas is available so do not worry if you run out. The owners live on the park to ensure the smooth running of the site. As a family site the owners ask for quite between 11pm and 7am and no loud radios, which ensures that everybody can have a peaceful holiday.

The children's play area has a large wooden climbing frame, complete with swing, money bars, and climbing wall and a 14ft trampoline. There is an indoor games room with pool table, table tennis, air hockey. A separate room accommodates a full size snooker table available for adults only.

Within the shop is a small take away where you can get Breakfast baps, burgers, chicken nuggets, scampi, and cod & chips. All food is cooked to order, and served during shop opening hours.

The Park is just over 15 miles from the Millennium Staduim in Cardiff. There is a local park & ride train service from Llantwit Major to the Staduim. Trains run every hour Monday to Saturday, and every two hours on Sundays.

'Crepe Night' on Saturday, Bank Holiday Weekend in August

Dogs are welcome on the following terms:

There is a charge of 75p per night for each dog.

Dogs must be on a lead at all times on the campsite.

It is a condition of your stay that you clean up after your dog immediately.

Dogs must not be left unattended on the campsite or in any vehicle.

Dogs are allowed onto the farm land outside the front gates.

By bringing your dog on to the park you are deemed to accept these terms.

Anyone found not to be clearing up after their dog, will be asked to leave.

Acorn Camping & Caravanning Access Statement:

Shop and reception access via ramp and wide doorway.

The whole site slopes gently towards the main entrance but is effectively quite level.

Touring pitches have a mix of grass and hard standings, and space for one car parked next to the caravan.

Tent pitches are grass and have parking for one car next to the tent.

Shower & toilet block has wide door access.

Separate purpose built unisex room with shower cubicle, toilet and basin with grab rails.

Access roads on the campsite are stone tracks with an uneven surface.

Guide dogs welcome.

Launderette is next to the dish washing area; with seating available.

Nearby facilities:

Local area:

There are so many places to visit within the area, from the spectacular Glamorgan coastline - Wales's first designated heritage coast, to the peace and tranquillity of the valleys with their fascinating history and industrial heritage.

Here are a few suggestions, of places you may like to visit:

Events in the Vale

Doctor Who Exhibition

Big Pit National Coal Museum

The National Showcaves

Folly Farm

Oakwood Theme Park

Llantwit Major History: Llantwit Major, or otherwise known as Llanilltud Fawr, has been occupied for over 3000 years. Bronze Age and Iron Age people, and the Romans lived here before the Celtic Church made this a place of national importance, but the oldest buildings now seen in the town were built by the Normans. The town square has at its centre an old preaching cross, which is now the war memorial. Around it is a group of Tudor buildings, built when the town had to be rebuilt following a visit with fire and sword by Owain Glyndwr shortly after 1400. About 1440, a new family came to Llantwit Major, the Raglans or Raglands. Robert Raglan built a house which is otherwise known as the Old White Hart public house, which makes it the oldest continually inhabited house in the town. Around 1465, Raglan built a new house, which in time was used by the church as a presbytery, and which in 1874 was extended and became the village school, now the "Old School" used by community groups. The Old Swan Inn on the other side of the square is another Raglan house. There is a tradition that this pub was at one time a mint. St. Illtud's Church, which was described by described by John Wesley in 1777 as "the most beautiful as well as the most spacious church in Wales", has a very long history. Christ has been worshipped here for about 1500 years, since Illtud came here and, by the side of the Ogney Brook, established a church, monastery and school. It became the burial place of local kings and an important mission centre. It contains one of the most significant collections of Celtic stones in Wales.

St. Fagans National History Museum: St Fagans is one of Wales's most popular Heritage attractions. It is located in the grounds of St. Fagans Castle, a late 16th century manor house. Over the last 50 years, more than 40 original buildings from different historical periods have been re-erected in the 100 acre parkland.   Buildings include different styles of Welsh houses throughout the ages, a farm, a chapel, school, craft workshops, and many more. There is also a large gallery, with exhibitions of costumes, daily life and farming implements. There are also special exhibitions which are held regularly. There is a self-service restaurant which is in the main building, with a snack-bar nearby. There is an award winning tea room which is definitely worth a visit is located above Gwalia Stores (open all year). Cafe Bardi is situated in the Main Entrance Hall and serves a variety of home-made cakes, sandwiches, boxed salads and soup and also hot and cold drinks. There is a picnic area just inside the open-air section, and the Museum's bakery also sells delicious bread and snacks.

Entry is free of charge.
Car park charge for the whole day.
Open hours are 10am-5pm

Castles:

Castle Coch on the outskirts of Cardiff, is the ultimate enchanting fairytale Castle. The Castle is rich in decoration, detail and allusion. Hidden away in beautiful woodlands, it overlooks the gorge in the Taff valley.

Caerphilly Castle is Wales largest moated Medieval Castle. The Fortress spreads over a hugh area of 30 acres. The castle is set in parkland in the middle of town.

Cardiff Castle is one of Wales's leading tourist attractions and is situated in the heart of the city centre. The Castle which dates back to Roman times was rebuilt and transformed in the 19th century into a medieval fantasy castle with lavish interiors.

Chepstow Castle, standing on the rocks above the River Wye, was built by the Normans *c* 1067 only one year after the landing at Hastings to guard the important river crossing; was the first stone built castle.

Further information can be obtained by clicking on the links on the Acorn Camping & Caravan Park website *Area Page.*

Activities:

With 28 miles of Stunning Coastline, which makes it perfect for water related sports, whether you choice is Surfing, Sea Fishing, Wind Surfing, or just relaxing on the Beach, while the kids play in the rock pools hunting for crabs & fish.

Inland from the coastal area are the Hills and Valleys, which offer Walking, Horse Riding, Quad Biking, Cycling, Lake Fishing and much more.

Information about: Activities, Beaches, Walking, Fishing, Surfing, Golf, Horse Riding and Millennium Stadium Events can be obtained by clicking on the links on the Acorn Camping & Caravan Park website *Activities Page.*

Rates: On application

Directions:

Please be aware when using most internet map searches and car satalite navigation systems that Acorn Camping & Caravan Park's post code does noy relate to their actual location. Furthermore, if you are towing do not go by the quickest route as the lanes may only be just wide enough for cars.

Satnav Co-ordinates are: +51° 23' 58.01", -3° 28' 40.91"

From the West (Swansea):

Leave the M4 at junction 35, Pencoed, follow the A473, and turn left onto the A48.

Turn right at Pentre Meyrick towards Llantwit Major on the B4268/4270.

After approx. 6 miles turn left at the first roundabout onto the B4265 towards Cardiff. *Do not* go straight across here towards Llantwit Major.

Straight across the mini roundabout.

At the lights turn right into Llanmaes Road under the railway bridge. Turn left at the first mini roundabout and left at the next mini roundabout.

Then turn right into Ham Lane East, between two sets of playing fields.

Follow this road past the school and over the speed bumps, you will then come to a sharp right hand turn, turn immediate left into Ham Manor Park. Follow the road straight on, and over the bridge. Turn a right and follow the road past the large roundabout, past the wooden chalet development on the right. Take a left and follow the road past the farm buildings. The Park is located at the top of the road on the left.

From the East (Cardiff):

Leave the M4 at junction 33 and follow the signs towards Cardiff International Airport. Then join the B4265 towards Llantwit Major.

At the third set of traffic lights, turn left, go under the railway-bridge and left at the first mini roundabout, then left at the next mini roundabout.

Then turn right into Ham Lane East, between two sets of playing fields.

Follow this road past the school and over the speed bumps, you will then come to a sharp right hand turn, turn immediate left into Ham Manor Park. Follow the road straight on, and over the bridge. Turn a right and follow the road past the large roundabout, past the wooden chalet development on the right. Take a left and follow the road past the farm buildings. The Park is located at the top of the road on the left.

Nearest town/resort: Llantwit Major

Out and about: Centrally situated for touring the Vale of Glamorgan and the Heritage Coast. To the west are the coastal attractions of Southerdown, Ogmore by Sea and Aberavon, while to the east are Barry and Penarth. Cardiff is only 15 miles away. St. Fagans National History Museum, just to the west of Cardiff is simply a must. The city itself is home to attractions too numerous to mention here. Castell Coch, known as 'The Fairy Castle', at Tongwynlais, is well worth a visit and so to is Caerphilly Castle – the second largest castle in Europe. If you are interested in pottery then you are in luck. You can visit the old pottery at Nantgarw near Caerphilly, and there are two working potteries to see, one at Rumney on the eastern side of Cardiff, and the other at Ewenny a just south of Bridgend. Take a trip to Bridgend and carry on up the valley along the A4061 through Ogmore Vale and over the Bwlch y Clawdd Pass to Treorcy in The Rhondda. Follow the road down through the valley through Porth and on to Trehafod, where you can visit the Rhondda Heritage Park at the old Lewis Merthyr colliery, then on to Pontypridd, and return to Llantwit Major via Llantrisant and Cowbridge.

The pub, A to B: Make your way to the town centre ¾ mile away, where you will discover a good selection of inns. Firstly, bear right out of the Park, then after 200 yards turn left into Ham Manor. After another 200 yards turn right into Mill Lay Lane, then, almost immediately, take the sharp left into Ham Lane South. Walk along for 600 yards to the junction with Colhugh Street. Here, turn right and follow up the street for another 250 yards to a fork in the road - take the right hand fork which will bring you out in East Street. Turn to the right and you will see the White Lion on your right hand side and the Kings Head more or less straight across the road on your left. After a well earned pint (or two), turn back down the street in the direction in which you came, and on into Church Street. You will find *The Old Swan Inn*; Llantwit Major's oldest pub, on your right – a CAMRA award winning pub…you'll like it! On leaving The Old Swan, and continuing a short distance along Church Street, then taking the right hand turning into Wine Street, you will come across The Old White Hart on the left hand side just at the beginning of the street.

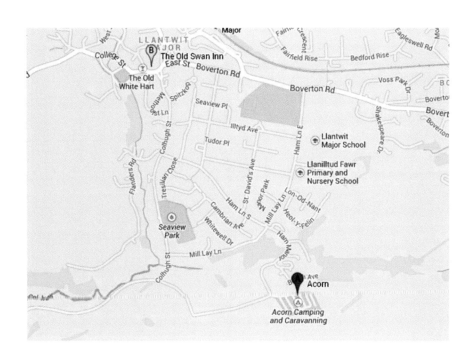

A. Acorn to B. The Old Swan Inn

Q. MONMOUTH

Monmouth Caravan Park
Rockfield Road
Monmouth
Monmouthshire
NP25 5BA
Tel: 01600 714745
Email: mail@monmouthcaravanpark.co.uk

Monmouth Caravan Park has no official website at present, information is however available at:
1. monmouth-caravan-park.wales.info
2. www.pitchup.com/campsites/Wales/South-Wales/Monmouthshire/Monmouth/monmouth-caravan-park/
3. www.caravanownersclub.co.uk/Site/Monmouth-Caravan-Park-NP25-5BA

Open: 1st March to 5th January

Pitches for: Monmouth Caravan Park is a family run site that offers 70 pitches, including 26 hard standings, for Touring Caravans, Motor Homes, Tents and Trailer Tents. All feature 10amp electric hook-up and are on firm level grass pitches.

Acreage: The 4 acre Park is situated in the ancient market and border town of Monmouth, close to the River Wye.

Access: Good

Site location: A quiet, friendly park owned by the Brown family, who live on the park itself. The park has been open since 1991. It is a perfect location for exploring the Wye Valley, Forest of Dean and Brecon Beacons. Monmouth is situated in the centre of an Area of Outstanding Natural Beauty. The views from the park are a delight and the town centre is an easy walk. For those looking for a more energetic holiday, the River Wye is close by and ideal for canoeing. Canoe hire is available locally, as is mountain bike hire. Offa's Dyke footpath is 75 metres from the site, while Monmouth town centre is just a stroll away.   The park has been open since 1991.

Facilities: Monmouth Caravan Park offers a basic toilet block, showers, hairdryer and a full disabled shower room.

On site there's a large bar area which has a pool table and serves food at the weekends, including Sunday breakfast.

On Saturday nights and bank holidays, evening entertainment is provided, as well as bingo.

Caravan storage facilities are available.

A run-down of the on-site facilities available include:

Family Friendly
Rallies Welcome
Gas Refills Available
Electric Hook-ups
Toilet Block
Washing Up
Chemical Disposal
Showers
Bar on Site
Restaurant/Café on Site
Local Produce
Disabled Facilities
Recycling Available

Dogs are welcome.

Nearby facilities:

Nearby amenities
Bar nearby
Nearby farmers' market
Public transport nearby
Shop nearby

Nearby leisure
Canoeing/kayaking nearby
Cycle hire nearby
Cycling nearby
FIshing nearby
Golf nearby
Horse riding nearby
Indoor pool nearby
Mountain biking nearby
Restaurant nearby
Tennis nearby
Watersports nearby

Rates: On application

Directions: From Monmouth take the B4233, the Park is ¼ mile on the right hand side, opposite the fire station.

Nearest town/resort: Monmouth

Out and about: Monmouth was the birthplace of Henry V, and Charles Rolls, co-founder of Rolls Royce. The town has many attractions for the visitor. Here is the Monnow Bridge, the only fortified Norman Bridge to survive in Britain. The castle was the birthplace of Henry the Fifth, whose statue, along with that of Charles Rolls, can be seen in Agincourt Square. The town also has close connections with Lord

Nelson, and the Nelson Museum houses many artefacts associated with him. A visit to the area is not complete without a trip down the A466 along the lower Wye Valley to the majestic ruins of the Cistercian Abbey at Tintern, and on to Chepstow to see the first castle the Normans began building in stone without first erecting a wooden structure. Chepstow races are well known to the horse racing fraternity, and the racecourse hosts a market every Sunday morning. Offa's Dyke can be traced from Chepstow all the way to Prestatyn, and for the serious walker The Offer's Dyke Footpath is quite a rewarding challenge.

The pub, A to B: Bearing left out of the Park into Watery Lane, and then turning left onto Rockfield Road, a short stroll of ¼ mile will bring you into the centre of Monmouth town, where you will find numerous hotels and public houses from which to choose. On your way in to town you will see The Three Horse Shoes on your right in Drybridge Street. After passing over the Monnow Bridge you will see The Gate House on the left immediately at the end of the bridge in Monnow Street. Just a little way up the street on your right you will find The Robin Hood. Walking to the top of the street you will reach Agincourt Square. *The Punch House* is straight in front of you…an old imposing inn with well-kept ale. If you turn to your left out of The Punch House and walk along the narrow Church Street turning right into St. Mary Street, down the street and left at the corner, you will see The Queens Head over the road to the right in St James' Street (the building itself is a Grade II listed building and dates back to around the Sixteenth Century). From The Queens Head continue your way along St. James' Street, and then bear right, 'the wrong way', around the one-way system, and right again into Old Dixton Road. The Old Nags Head is a few yards further on the right on the corner of Granville Street.

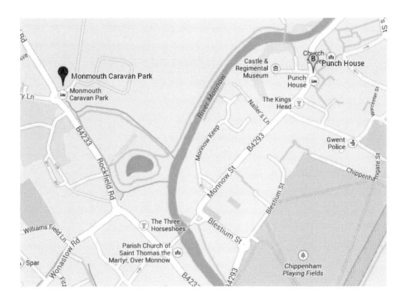

A. The Caravan Park to B. The Punch House

R. NARBERTH

Noble Court Holiday Park
Redstone Road
Narberth
Pembrokeshire
SA67 7ES
Tel: 01834 861908
www.celticholidayparks.com/Noble_Court_holiday_park/index.htm
Email: Please use the email form on the Celtic Holiday Park website *Contact Page*

Open: 1st March to 31st October

Pitches for: Noble Court has 92 level/sloping touring pitches for tents, touring caravans and motor caravans; and a camping field. Hard and grass pitches are available. There are pitches with electric hook-up available, and also a small number of pitches with no utilities. The Park has 60 static caravan holiday homes of which 4 are available for rent.

Acreage: Set in 40 acres of rolling countryside

Access: Good

Site location: Close to the heart of Pembrokeshire life but away from the hustle and bustle of the main tourist spots, Noble Court combines peace and quiet with easy access to a host of attractions and facilities. Although surrounded by lovely countryside so typical of inland Pembrokeshire the Park is less than half a mile from the old market town of Narberth with its exquisite boutiques, glorious galleries, great restaurants and fine selection of specialist shops.

Facilities:

Noble Court's facilities include:
Celtic Bar with patio.
Outdoor heated swimming pool and splash pool (open 9 to 5 Whitsun week to end August (subject to change) under 16's require supervision).
Well-stocked coarse fishing lake (licence and permit required).
Two adventure playgrounds.
Football pitch.
Games room and amusement arcade.

All the facilities of the Park are available to Tourers and Campers, with the addition of the following specific facilities:
Hard and grass pitches for touring caravans, motorhomes and tents
Electric hook-ups
Separate grass areas
Shower and toilet facilities
Free hot water to shower
Plentiful water points
Wash-up areas

Dogs are welcome

Nearby facilities:
Shops and evening entertainment – Narberth, half a mile
Beach 5 miles
Close to Oakwood Theme Park and Folly Farm Family Adventure Park
Golf
Fishing
Sailing
Boating
Horse riding
Water skiing
Tennis…
all close by

The Pembrokeshire Countryside:
Pembrokeshire is without doubt, a true gem of a holiday destination. For a start, it boasts Britain's only coastal National Park featuring nearly 200 miles of soaring headlands, sheltered coves, sheer cliffs, sweeping sandy beaches and peaceful estuaries – all protected and abounding with wonderful wildlife.

Guide to Activities:
There's so much to discover in Pembrokeshire. Manorbier's beach-side castle is close by as are a host of top-quality beaches. To the far west, you'll find St. David's with its impressive cathedral founded by the patron saint of Wales. Fishguard offers splendid views over a busy harbour and the opportunity for that 'edge of the world' feeling with a visit to Strumble Head.

Pembrokeshire's Attractions:
Pembrokeshire has a whole host of diverse attractions to suit all ages.

Wet Weather Attractions:
Pembrokeshire is full of exciting attractions and fun days even when the sun is not shining.

Pembrokeshire Weather and Tides:
It is always good to know what weather is likely to greet you before you go on holiday (and while you're away if you have access to a computer!) whether it's for a last minute short break or a long-planned main holiday.

For further information… visit the Celtic Holiday Park's website 'About Pembrokeshire Page' and follow the links

Rates: On application

Directions: Westbound from the M4 – at the end of the M4, follow the A48 for Carmarthen. At Carmarthen, follow the A40 to the first roundabout after Llanddewi Velvrey and take the second exit signed A40. Take the first turning on your left signed B4313 Narberth & Noble Court. The Park is situated a third of a mile from the junction on the left hand side.

Nearest town/resort: Narberth

Out and about: A friendly site close to beaches and mountains - an ideal base for touring Pembrokeshire. The popular seaside resorts of Saundersfoot and Tenby are close by. A short distance away is Whitland where you can visit the Hywel Dda Memorial Gardens. Pembertons' Chocolates and Llanboidy Cheese are made at Llanboidy a little to the north of Whitland, and you are able to visit both of these establishments. Two great attractions for the children are Oakwood Theme Park and Folly Farm Family Adventure Park – both close by.

For those interested in castles, Pembroke Castle with its large natural cavern (the Wogan) under the keep, is well worth a visit. Another place well worth visiting is St. Govan's Chapel at St. Govans head, which is to the south of Pembroke. The cliffs here are quite spectacular.

The pub, A to B: Once you've turned left out of the Park you only have to take a gentle stroll down Redstone Road for ½ mile into Narberth, where you can take your pick from a selection of good inns. The first you will come across is ***The Farmers Arms*** on your left on the corner of Northfield Road - a nice pub, with a nice atmosphere. On coming out of The Farmers, make your way over the road into High Street. As you go down the street you will find The Coach and Horses, The Ivy Bush and the Angel Hotel on your left, all waiting to greet you. Carry along down - High Street runs into Water Street. The Eagle Inn and The Dragon Inn are both at the bottom of the street on your right.

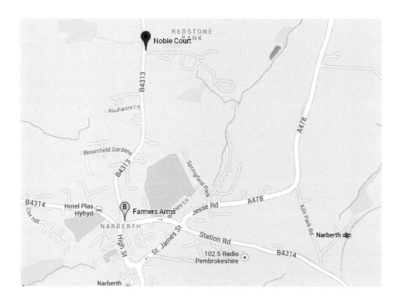

A. Noble Court to B. The Farmers Arms

S. NEWPORT, PEMBBROKESHIRE

Tycanol Farm Camping
Newport
Pembrokeshire
SA42 0ST
Tel: 01239 820264

Tycanol Farm Camping has no official website at present, information is however available at:
1. www.caravancampingsites.co.uk/pembrokeshire/tycanolfarm.htm
2. www.pitchup.com/campsites/Wales/South-Wales/Pembrokeshire/Newport/tycanol-farm-camping/
3. www.coolcamping.co.uk/campsites/uk/wales/west-wales/pembrokeshire/1052-tycanol-farm

Open: All year

Pitches for: Tycanol Farm Camping has ample space with 60 pitches for tents, touring caravans and motorhomes (4 hardstandings) as well as a bunk-house (sleeps 4). The pitches are level and well sheltered.

Acreage: The 6 acre site which is part of Tycanol Farm is situated on the coastal path.

Access: Good

Site location: A perfectly located site slap-bang on Britain's only coastal national park with easy access to beaches and the town. Tycanol is an Organic farm. The nearest beach is a 2 minute walk and the peaceful town of Newport is a short 20 minute stroll away.
There is hardly a campsite in The British Isles that can beat this one for views! The Pembrokeshire Coast National Park is right on Tycanol's doorstep. Weaving its way across 186 miles of some of the most thrilling coastal scenery to be found anywhere in Europe; from Amroth in the south to St. Dogmel's in the north, this epic journey covers just about every kind of seaside landscape…from soft sandy beaches and craggy cliffs to meandering estuaries and shady coves.
Newport, with its laid back way of life, stands beneath Carn Ingli. The charming streets of the town lead down to the estuary of the River Nevern (Afon Nyfer) which teems with wildlife.

Facilities: An ideal base from which to tour South West Wales; Tycanol Farm is a well maintained site whose basic facilities include:
Pitches for Tents, Touring Caravans and Motorhomes
4 Hard Standings
Electric Hook-ups
Bunk House - sleeps 4
Toilets
Hot Showers
Chemical Disposal Point

Dish-washing
Freezer
Children's Play Area
Launderette
Free BBQ held nightly
Beach
Fishing
Nice Views
Local Leaflets

Dogs are welcome

Nearby Facilities: The following off-site amenities are available locally:

Food Shop - 1 mile
Gas – 1 mile
Bar/Pub – 500 yards
Restaurant – 500 yards
Takeaway Food – 1 mile
Indoor Heated Pool – 10 miles
Tennis Courts – 1 mile

Activities include…
Golf
Fishing
Sailing
Boating
Horse riding
Water Skiing
Tennis
Climbing

If it rains…
St. David's Cathedral
Castell Henllys Iron Age Village
Day trip to Ireland from Fishgaurd

Rates: On application

Directions: A487 from Fishguard - 7miles to Newport. A487 from Cardigan -12 miles to Newport.
Tycanol Farm is on the Fishguard side of Newport and 1 mile from the town.
You are advised *not to use Sat Nav* beyond Newport as it takes you down a narrow lane.

Nearest town/resort: Newport

Out and about: Newport was the birthplace of probably the most notorious pirate of them all – Bartholamew Roberts – aka –'Black Bart'. Overlooking Newport is Carn

Ingli (Place of Angels), a 1138 feet outer of the Prescellys. On its slopes are the remains of an iron-age fort and pre Christian hut circles. Situated near Newport is Pentre Ifan, a 5000 year old megalithic long barrow said to be the finest of its kind in Britain. Pay a visit to nearby Nevern Church to see the Vitialanus Stone, inscribed in Latin and 5th century Ogham script, which is situated near the porch. To the east of the porch stands St. Brynach's Cross, which probably dates from the 10th century. Leading up to the church is a dark avenue of gnarled old yew trees, one of which drops a blood-like sap and is known as the bleeding yew. Nearby Castell Henllys, an ancient Celtic fortified settlement is well worth visiting. Much excavation and restoration work has been done on the site – enough to give you an idea of what living conditions were like back in the iron- age. A journey through the Gwaun Valley along the B4313 to the south east of Fishguard returning to Newport along the B4329 and A487 is something that should not be missed.

The pub, A to B: A short stroll of approaching a quarter of a mile from the Campsite will bring you to the main road. Turn left there, and stroll a further three quarters of a mile into Newport, or Trefdraeth as it is in Welsh. There are four hostelries for you to try. First up on your left is The Royal Oak in West Street. Just along the way, still on your left but now in Bridge Street, is The Castle Inn. Crossing over the road and moving on into East Street you will find The Llwyngwair Arms on the right hand side. And last but not least, on the left and still in East Street, is *The Golden Lion*. I have fond memories of an enjoyable evening spent at this excellent hostelry…but I am not about to share them with you!

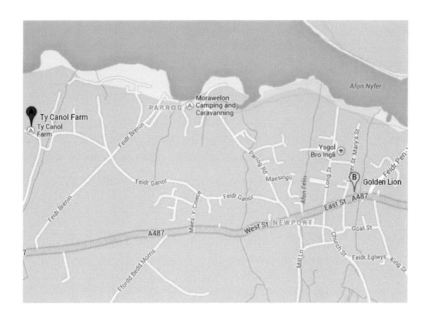

A. Tycanol to B. The Golden Lion

T. PORT EYNON

Carreglwyd Caravan & Camping Site
The Seafront
Port Eynon
Gower
Swansea
SA3 1NN
Tel: 01792 390795 - **9am – 5pm.**
Enquiries by telephone only please.
www.porteynon.com

Open: All year

Pitches for: Carreglwyd Caravan & Camping has 400 pitches to accommodate caravans, motorhomes and tents, in five well-drained and maintained fields. Electric pitches are available and are allocated upon arrival.

Acreage: The 15 acre site is located at the edge of Port Eynon village adjacent to the beach.

Access: Good

Site location: Carreglwyd is a busy, beach-side Park on the South Gower Coast, overlooking the picturesque village and Bay of Port Eynon. The fifteen acre site is surrounded by steep cliffs to one side and magnificent coastline on the other. Direct access to the beach makes this the perfect location for families, particularly those with young children. An ideal location for touring the beautiful Gower Peninsula, which is designated 'an Area of Outstanding Natural Beauty', and the nearby city of Swansea.

Facilities: On-site facilities include:

The 400 pitches are non-marked or specified, enabling visitors to choose their own spot in relation to the facilities and the beach.

Electric pitches are allocated upon arrival.

Two modern sanitary blocks serve the Park which comprise of toilets, showers, laundry and dish-washing areas.

There is also an outdoor wetsuit shower area.

All daily needs are catered for at the on-site shop, groceries, camping accessories, hardware, beach goods and off-licence as well as gas bottles and appliances.

Direct access to the beach makes this the perfect location for families, particularly those with young children.

Also, for those who need to keep in touch, free Wi-Fi is available.

Dogs are welcome. All dogs must be kept on a short lead, cleaned up after, and not left unattended on site at any time.

Nearby facilities:

The beach has lifeguard cover during the summer months, and the bay is ideal for bathing, fishing and a variety of water sports.

The Gower Peninsula is little more than fifteen miles long and five miles wide, and is unique; the coastal scenery is unsurpassed - rugged limestone cliffs and rock-bound shores alternate with splendid sandy bays, each with its own characteristic and individual allure. The almost insular character of Gower has been the main factor in the preservation of the old-world atmosphere which appeals to so many of its visitors.

Port Eynon is the perfect starting point for exploring the area, whether by car, bicycle or on foot. The cliff walk to Rhossili (7miles) via Mewslade and Fall Bay is unrivalled in the grandeur of its unspoilt scenery, and should be undertaken by every visitor.

The City of Swansea is 18 miles away by road and is connected to Port Eynon by an (almost) hourly bus service, or a drive yourself, will take around 40 minutes.

Rates: On application

Directions:

From M4 (East) travelling westbound:
Leave motorway Junction 42 M4 joining A483 to Swansea.

From Swansea follow A4118 to Port Eynon (18 miles)

Warning: Do not use Sat Nav systems in Gower. These will lead you down some very narrow lanes.
Stay on main road A4118. Do not deviate. Carreglwyd is at the end of this road.
Gower roads are narrow in places, please drive carefully.
The Site is closed to all traffic between 11pm & 8am.

Nearest town/resort: Swansea

Out and about: An ideal location for touring the beautiful Gower Peninsula, which is designated 'an Area of Outstanding Natural Beauty', and the nearby city of Swansea. On the Gower there are beaches, bays, and coves; and more beaches, bays, and coves…… No visit to Swansea can be complete without a visit to its market, famous for its food produce. Treat yourself to some Penclawdd cockles – they're delicious! Travel from Swansea up the valley on the A4067 for fifteen miles to visit the spectacular Dan yr Ogof show-caves. While you are at it, pay a visit to the highest waterfall in South Wales, Henrhyd Falls at Coelbren – you can actually stand underneath the cataract. Take a trip west to Llanelli, home of the famous 'Scarlets' rugby team; then on to Burry Port where, Amelia Earhart, who was the first woman to fly the Atlantic, landed. Visit the 12 golden miles of Cefn Sidan Sands and the magnificent ruins of Kidwelly Castle. To the east of Swansea, Neath Abbey and the Aberdulais Falls are both well worthy of a visit.

The pub, A to B: Port Eynon has only the one pub, *The Ship Inn*…a cosy, local pub within 5 minutes' walk of the Campsite, so you will have no trouble finding it. Bear left after leaving the Campsite and take the second turning right. The Ship is on your left.

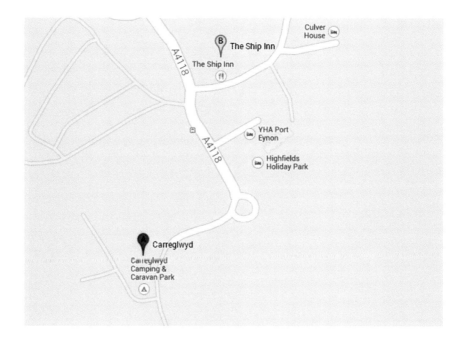

A. Carreglwyd to B. The Ship Inn

U. RHAYADER

Wyeside Caravan & Camping Park
Llangurig Road
Rhayader
Powys
LD6 5LB
Tel: 01597 810 183
www.wyesidecamping.co.uk
Email: wyesidecc@powys.gov.uk

Open: March until the last day of October for touring and camping.

Static caravans can be used from February until November inclusive.

Motorhomes and touring caravans with their own on board facilities can be accommodated in February and November; please phone to check availability before arrival due to the unknown nature of the weather in these two months!

Closed in both December and January; however, bookings for the next season are still welcome in these months.

Pitches for: Wyeside has 40 pitches available for Touring Caravans. Both grass and hardstanding seasonal touring pitches are available as well as units for visitors staying for just one night or more. All of the touring pitches have electric hook-ups and television hook-up facilities.

There are 100 spaces available for Tents at Wyeside in the camping field. Touring Caravans and Camper Vans are also welcomed into this area. There are a limited amount of electric hook-ups in this field.

The Statics Caravans at Wyeside are privately owned. Occasionally there are vans for sale on site but due to the stunning location and the friendly atmosphere these get snapped up quickly. Contact the Park us if you would like to know more about owning a caravan at Wyeside.

Acreage: The Park comprises 8 acres of level touring pitches covering 2 separate areas.

Access: Good

Site location: Located in the old market town of Rhayader Wyeside Caravan and Campsite is just a short drive away from the Elan Valley Dams where you can witness some of the most spectacular scenery that Powys has to offer.

The Park is situated on the banks of the River Wye just a short 400 yards walk to Rhayader's town centre,

The bijou town of Rhayader offers visitors impressive architecture inclusive of their four faced town clock, cosy and welcoming tea and coffee shops, a small supermarket, local produce retailers and a well-equipped Leisure Centre

Facilities: The site offers its guests use of the two modern shower and toilet blocks, a laundrette and small well equipped shop.

The Camping Field is serviced by its own large toilet and shower block with disabled facilities.   There are a limited amount of electric hook-ups in the field. Other facilities available on site and near to the Camping Field are pot washing and launderette.

The Touring Caravans area is served by its own toilet and shower block with disabled access and facilities. This block also offers its users in the Touring area a pot wash and chemical disposal unit. All of the touring pitches have electric hook-ups and television hook-up facilities.

Static Caravan facilities include:
Electric Hook Up points (all)
Television Ariel points (Tourers)
Large clean toilet and shower block (all)
Disabled access to facilities (all)
Pot washing station (all)
Chemical disposal units (all)
Launderette (all)
Reception (all)

The River Wye runs through the site and is ideal for canoeing and fishing, further details on fishing can be found at www.rhayaderangling.co.uk or click on the link on the Wyeside website *The Site Page (About Us).*

It is an ideal holiday centre for young and old alike, for nature enthusiasts, walkers and lovers of tranquil and outstanding scenery, or those just wanting to get away from it all.

Dogs are welcome. Dogs must be kept under control and on a lead at all times.

Nearby facilities:

Waun Capel Parc which adjoins the camping field boasts a bowling green (one of the best in Wales), tennis courts, putting golf, playing field and a children's park.

Things to See and Do in Powys… visit www.exploremidwales.co.uk, or click on the link on the Wyeside website *Out and About Page.*

Local Towns, Activities and Places to Eat… click on the links on the Wyeside website *Out and About Page.*

Rates: On application

Directions: Getting to Wyeside is easy - the Park is 400 yards north of Rhayader on the A470.

Nearest town/resort: Rhayader

Out and about: Wyeside is ideally situated for visiting the Elan Valley, which is just 3 miles away. The valley contains a chain of four large reservoirs, and the picturesque hill scenery of this 'Welsh Lake District' is well known and can be reached most easily by the B4518 from Rhayader. A must for all wildlife enthusiasts is a visit to Gigrin Farm on the edge of the town to see the Red Kites being fed (every day at 2 pm GMT). The elegant spa town of Llandrindod Wells is only 7 miles away. It hosts its famous Victorian Festival each August, when locals and visitors alike, dress up in Victorian costumes and take to the streets. 15 miles to the south at Cilmery is the roadside monument to Llywelyn ap Gruffydd the last of the native princes of Wales; whilst 10 miles to the north east are the ruins of Abbey Cwm Hir where Llywelyn's body was laid to rest, and a gravestone commemorates the fact. Rhayader was one of the centres of the Rebecca Riots in the nineteenth century, when men dressed themselves as women and calling themselves Rebecca's Daughters smashed the turnpike gates as a protest against the heavy tolls. The town once had a castle, but all that is left of it now is a large mound and a few stones standing high above the River Wye.

The pub, A to B: Rhayader is renowned for being the town with the highest concentration of pubs and drinking establishments, per capita, in the UK with one to each 173 people.
Leave the Camping Field via the 'back way' in the far right hand corner away from the main entrance next to the river which is on your right hand side. After climbing over the style you are now in Waun Capel Parc. Pass by the bowling green, playing field and children's play area to where the path forks away in two directions. Make a mental note of the path that leads off in front of you and in an upward direction, as you will be returning this way. But for now, take the path which bears off to the right following the course of the river. This will bring you out in Bridge Street where you should turn to your right and cross over the bridge into Llansantffraed Cwmdeuddwr. Within 75 yards or so of the bridge follow the lane which leads off left down to ***The Triangle Inn.*** This is a beautiful 16th century Drovers Inn overlooking the River Wye – a real gem! When you've finished in The Triangle make your way back over the bridge into Rhayader. Walking along Bridge Street up into West Street you will see The Cornhill Inn on the left and just after it ***The Elan Hotel*** on the right, then back on the left is The Lion Royal Hotel. You will now come to the Town Clock crossroads where West Street meets East Street, meets North Street, meets South Street – with

the Town Clock in the middle. Cross over the road into East Street and the Castle Hotel is on the left hand corner at the start of the street, then 400 yards along on the same side is the Bears Head. Returning back along East Street towards the Clock you will see the Royal Oak on the left hand side of the street. On arriving at the Clock, with The Castle on the corner, turn right into North Street. *The Lamb and Flag Inn* is only 25 yards along on the right. *The Crown Inn* is directly opposite on the other side…with a classic beamed interior and a comfortable traditional welcome. Further up North Street on the other side of the road to Smithfield Market is The Black Lion. And just a little further up the street from the Black Lion, as you're heading out of town, turn left and left again into Church Street, and the Eagles Inn is there on your right. From The Eagles carry on down the street and take the first turning on your right into Castle Road, through the gate, back into Waun Capel Parc, and down the path which will lead you back to whence you came at the start of the walk.

This is quite a pub-crawl! It may be prudent to limit yourself to visiting just a small number of these hostelries, say…*The Triangle, The Elan Hotel, The Lamb and Flag* and *The Crown*

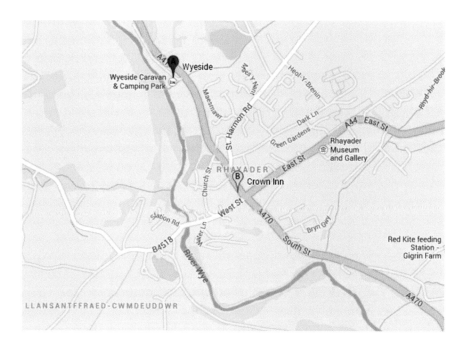

A. Wyeside to B. The Crown Inn

V. ST. DAVIDS

Caerfai Bay Caravan & Tent Park
Caerfai Bay
St. Davids
Haverfordwest
Pembrokeshire
SA62 6QT
Tel: 01437 720274
You are advised to telephone between 8.30 a.m. and 4 p.m. Monday to Saturday, or Sunday between 9 a.m. and noon if possible. There is always an answer phone.
Fax: 01437 720577
www.caerfaibay.co.uk
Email: Use the email form on the Caerfai Bay website *Contact Page*

Open: March to the second week of November

Pitches for: 109 level/sloping touring pitches for tents, touring caravans and motor caravans.
Caerfai Bay Caravan and Tent Park consists of three separate enclosures: The Caravan Park is licensed for 60 caravans. Approximately 25 are touring pitches, all with hook-ups and 17 with hardstandings: The remainder are season site pitches, of which 9 are for hire. Field 2 and field 3 are for tent and motor homes. These have ample electric hook-ups and some hardstandings. Motor homes without awnings may stay in the caravan field – subject to caravan rates either in the off season, or during the School Summer holidays if they have a dog. (Note – dogs not allowed in the tent field during the School Summer holidays).

Acreage: The Park covers approximately 9 acres in all with panoramic coastal views overlooking St. Brides Bay.

Access: Good

Site location: The Pembrokeshire Coastal Path is adjacent to the site entrance with Caerbwdy Bay a short walk to the east and St. Non's Chapel to the west. St. Davids and its shops are a ten minute walk away, just under a mile.

Facilities: The Park is open from the first of March to the second week of November for touring caravans, tents and motor homes.
There are nine static caravans for hire.

Amenities:
Free Hot Showers
Family Amenity Block
ElectricShaver Points
Electric Hook-up Points
Public Telephone
Camping Gaz & Calor Gas

Launderette Including Iron & Board
Dish Washing Rooms
Hairdryers
Internet
Disabled Toilet & Shower

The facilities are located in two areas:

Caravan field complex: situated at the top of the caravan field, is the Park Office (where you can buy bottled gas, post cards etc.) and adjacent disabled toilet/shower. An amenity building described on the Caerfai Bay website *Home Page > Amenities Room,* and includes The Launderette, Dishwash, Kitchen, Phone Charging Bank, Internet Facility, Rest Area an Information. Although this facility is provided at the Caravan Park end, it is for the use of all Visitors on the Park.

A separate block with telephone kiosk, grey and chemical waste cubicles, unisex toilets and wet suit wash is immediately opposite. Outside are the grey and chemical dump stations for motor homes.

Tent field complex: (between the caravan field and first tent field): Men's and Ladies toilet/shower block, dishwash room, a small kitchen and wet suit wash room. Also family amenity units – two of which have small baths/shower, baby changers, basin and toilet, – and two with shower, basin and toilet.

Disabled facilities:

Since 2001 there have been some disabled facilities installed on the Park. These include ramps to the site office and a purpose built shower/toilet facility. The whole of the Park has panoramic sea views. Although the Park cannot cater for disabled groups, individuals or families with a disabled member are welcomed.

Unfortunately Caerfai beach itself is not accessible for wheelchairs, however there are some local places such as Whitesands, which is a popular and accessible beach that sees a lot of activity during the summer. At Abereiddy a few miles further north there is a wheelchair friendly coastal path that starts from the beach car park.

Recycling and non-recycled waste facilities:

At the top of the caravan field
Below the tent field amenity complex

Dogs are welcome. Dogs are allowed on site but must be kept on a lead at all times, however, during the School Summer holiday period the tent fields are dog-free areas, i.e. Tents and Motor Homes in fields 2 an 3 should not have dogs. Normally dogs would be exercised off site – on the adjacent cliff path walk, but there is a small dog walk area next to the Park entrance which is handy for the emergency or short morning exercise!

Nearby facilities:

Attractions in and around Caerfai Bay:

Caerfai Bay Caravan and Tent Park is situated in a beautiful part of Wales, with views into Caerfai Bay and across St. Brides Bay towards Solva, Newgale, Broad Haven and the islands of Skomer, Skokholm, Grassholm and Ramsey.

Caerfai Bay: is a tidal beach: beautiful sands and fascinating rock pools when the tide is out. There is a concrete path down to the beach, some steps at the end, and depending on the sand level at the time of year, a few stones and pebbles just before the sand. There are many other beaches to visit locally such as Whitesands, Porth Melgan and Abereiddy. The Pembrokeshire Coast Path is approximately 180 miles long. You can take a short walk from the beach or for the more serious walker try the whole length. In recent years small local bus services have been developed to connect various stages of the walk.

Recommended websites can be found by clicking on the links on the Caerfai Bay website *Local Attractions Page.*

Whitesands: has a wide expanse of sand, suitable for surfing, swimming and kayaking. It has a permanent lifeguard station, café and shop.

Porth Melgan: is approached by cliff paths to the north of Whitesands, and is en route to St. Davids Head where there are some stone circles – remnants of a Neolithic settlement, and also a Neolithic burial chamber called a Cromlech.

Porth Selau: is another small beach approached this time from the southern path from Whitesands.

Abereiddy: beach is known for its dark sand and fossils. Cottage ruins and ruins of old quarry workings can be seen on the footpath (part of which has wheelchair access) and takes you to 'The Blue Lagoon' a flooded quarry to the north of Abereiddy.

Local Harbours: Porthclais, Solva, Abercastle and ***Porthgain*** (where you can see the remnants of old granite workings; it also has a pub – 'The Sloop', and a seafood Bistro – 'The Shed'.

St. Justinian: not only houses the Lifeboat station, but several of the boat trips to Ramsey and the outer islands go from here.

Recommended websites can be found by clicking on the links on the Caerfai Bay website *Local Attractions Page.*

Outside activities:

Outside activity adventures such as coasteering, climbing, kayaking and surfing can be arranged from *TYF in St. Davids.*

To explore the peninsula by horseback, you can go to the *St. Davids Trekking Centre.* A different day out can be had discovering some of the edible delights of our shoreline and hedgerows with *Really Wild Foraging.*

Indoor activities:

There are swimming pools and leisure centres in Fishguard and Haverfordwest. There is a new local sports hall in St. Davids near the school.

For more information click on the links on the Caerfai Bay website *Local Attractions Page.*

Cultural attractions:

Oriel y Parc, this is a new gallery and landscape interpretation centre at the top of Caerfai Road in St. Davids.

St. Davids Cathedral.

St. Davids Bishops Palace: This is located in the valley on the other side of the River Alun from the Cathedral. It is an ancient monument in the care of CADW.

For more information click on the links on the Caerfai Bay website *Local Attractions Page.*

Pembrokeshire is fortunate to have outstanding natural attractions such as beaches and coastal scenery.

There is also a wealth of activities for families:
Celtic Quest Coasteering
Blue Lagoon Water Park
Folly Farm
Zorbing
BP Karting
Heatherton
The Dinosaur Park
Anna's Welsh Zoo
Oakwood Theme Park
Pembroke Castle
Haverfordwest Town Museum

For more information click on the links on the Caerfai Bay website *Local Attractions Page.*

Rates: On application

Directions:

From Haverfordwest: take the A487 to St. Davids, at the entrance to St. Davids, turn left at Oriel y Parc/St. Davids visitor centre. 'Caerfai' is sign posted.
Alternative route: avoiding the hills of Newgale and Solva, take the A40 to Letterston, then B4331 to join the Fishguard Road to St. Davids A487 near Mathry.

From Fishguard: take the A487 to St. Davids, once in the city, turn left at Barclays Bank, up the High Street and past the Grove Hotel, turn at Oriel y Parc/Visitor Centre. 'Caerfai' is sign posted

Nearest town/resort: St. Davids

Out and about: The site is only ¾ mile from St. Davids, Wales' smallest city. A visit to the cathedral dedicated to Wales' patron saint is a must. To Welshmen this is the most hallowed spot in the British Isles. The cathedral and its ancillary buildings are almost hidden in the vale of the River Alun. It is thought that the building was especially tucked away like this so that pirates and invaders would not see it. Nonetheless it has been wrecked many times. Another must is a visit to St. Non's Chapel, above St. Non's Bay. Non was David's mother; and it was at this spot that David is reputed to have been born. Opinions differ as to St. David's birthdate, but he is said to have died in AD601 at the age of 147. St. David's Peninsula is a fascinating place to explore. This is a windswept and almost treeless land where the Pembrokeshire Coast Path runs along magnificent cliff tops. Seals breed in this area, and are frequently seen. Abereiddy, St. David's Head, Porthgain, Solfa and Whitesands Bay are all worthy of visiting.

The pub, A to B: On leaving the Campsite and bearing left, make your way steadily up Ffordd Caerfai to St. Davids, less than ¾ mile away. The tiny city does not boast an over-abundance of hostelries. Near the top of Ffordd Caerfai you will see a turning which goes off to your left into Feidr Pant y Bryn, in front of Oriel y Parc. Follow this turning then bear to the right 100 yards along. You are now at the junction with High Street. Up the road to your right, and some 30 yards away on the other side, you will find The Grove Hotel. Returning back down the road from the Grove, carry straight ahead for the city centre. At the end of High Street is Cross Square. On your right hand side as you go down onto the Square you will see The Old Cross Hotel, and across the Square, The Bishops. Goat Street, or Stryd yr Afr, leads off down from the bottom left of the Square. Barely 100 yards down Goat Street on the right hand side you will find *The Farmers Arms*. I always enjoy the ambience of The Farmers...it's hard to come to St David's and not pop in for a pint or two.

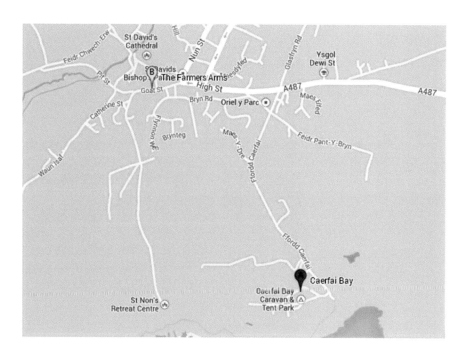

A. Caerfai Bay to B. The Farmers Arms

W. TREARDDUR BAY

Bagnol Caravan Park
Ravenspoint Road
Trearddur Bay
Anglesey
LL65 2AX
Tel: 01407 860223
www.caravan-park-anglesey.co.uk
Email: Use the email form on the Bagnol Caravan Park website *Contact Information Section*

Bagnol Caravan Park *and* **Tyn Towyn Caravan Park** *are close to each other and are set in their own grounds in Trearddur Bay*

Bagnol Caravan Park:
Touring caravan park & motorcaravans
Separate area for camping (tents)
Static caravans for sale

Tyn Towyn Caravan Park:
Static caravans for sale

Open: 1st March to end October

Pitches for: The Touring Park is located on Bagnol Caravan Park and has 113 pitches in total (touring caravans and camping combined). Level touring pitches for tents, touring caravans and motor caravans.
For touring caravans there are hard standings with electricity and water, and there is street lighting over the whole area. There is also a caravan storage facility for storing caravans over the winter.
Static caravans on site are not for hire (on a weekly basis etc.), but are for sale only for siting on the Park, and must be purchased through the owners or their agents.
Self-catering holiday cottages are available for hire.

Acreage: The Touring Park occupies 11acres in a rural location in Trearddur Bay.

Access: Good

Site location: Bagnol Caravan Park and Tyn Towyn Caravan Park are both set in their own grounds within walking distance of the marvellous sandy beach at Trearddur Bay. Situated on Holy Island near Holyhead with easy access from the new A55 dual carriageway across Anglesey.
The Caravan Parks are conveniently located within easy walking distance of all beach facilities, local shops, public inns and restaurants.
The Caravan Parks are an ideal location for a holiday in North Wales, for touring the beautiful Isle of Anglesey, or as a location for your own static caravan.
They are ideally placed to have a rest-over period prior to departure or arrival on the ferry link to Dublin in Ireland via the ferry from Holyhead.

Facilities:

For Touring Caravans, Motor Homes and Tents:

Bagnol Caravan Park, where the Touring Park is located, has 113 pitches in total (touring caravans and camping combined).
For touring caravans there are hard standings with electricity and water.
There is street lighting over the whole area.
There are clean and modern facilities in the new toilet block featuring toilets and showers (including those for the disabled).
A laundrette and ironing facilities.
There is a Foodzone with a few vending machines for drinks and snacks.
There is also a caravan storage facility for storing caravans over the winter.

For Static Caravans:

Bagnol Caravan Park has 161 pitches for static caravans. The site enjoys an open aspect with views towards the sea.

Tyn Towyn Caravan Park is in a pleasant secluded location and is smaller with 50 static caravans. All caravans are set within rock outcrops with bushes and beautiful natural settings.

The caravan parks provide modern facilities to each caravan including:
Piped gas
Water
Drainage
Electric (16 Amp supply)

Self Catering Cottages are available for hire – details can be obtained by clicking on the link on the Bagnol and Tyn Towyn website *Home Page*

No Dogs on the Touring Site due to health and safety regulations.

Nearby facilities: The Caravan Parks are conveniently located within easy walking distance of all beach facilities, local shops, public inns and restaurants.

The Parks are close to *interesting coves* and *sandy beaches,* which are renowned throughout the UK for swimming, sunbathing, snorkelling and sub aqua diving. The main beach has a *Blue Flag rating* for cleanliness and clarity of water.

There are *numerous activities* to enjoy in the area including boating, fishing, walking and horse riding.

There is a large *boating* regatta during each August and the caravan parks are very convenient for those wanting to watch or participate.

Boats can be easily launched from Trearddur Bay. The caravan park offers secure storage facilities where clients can leave their fishing/ski boats on a yearly or short term basis. Nearby Holyhead is an all year round deep harbour for yachting enthusiasts and motor boats.

This area of Anglesey is ideal for *sea fishing* and people wishing to fish can do so from the surrounding rocks and fresh bait is easily available from local suppliers on a daily basis.

For those who enjoy *walking* there are many splendid walks over the headlands following footpaths that start at Bagnol Caravan Park. These footpaths are suitable for the young and old alike.

Horse riding is also popular in the area, and there are local stables where you can hire a horse.

For those who enjoy *golf* there is an 18 hole course at Holyhead Golf Club (1.5 miles away), and a 9 hole course a few hundred yards from Tyn Towyn Caravan Park with easy access from Bagnol Touring Park.

There are numerous *tourist attractions* on the Isle of Anglesey to be visited on your holiday including South Stack Lighthouse, Anglesey Sea Zoo, Beaumaris Castle, Henblas Park, and many historical Celtic monuments.
A fantastic evening sight is the setting of the sun across the bay which has inspired many poets and artists. The area is an artist's paradise in which many local and professional artists have found inspiration from the beautiful landscape and surroundings.

Rates: On application

Directions: Follow the A55 Expressway across Anglesey. Leave the A55 at junction 3 and follow signs (A5) for Valley. Turn left at Valley onto the B4545 for Trearddur Bay.
For Bagnol Caravan Park turn left into Ravenspoint Road. After 1 mile, turn left into the Park.
For Tyn Towyn Caravan Park turn left opposite The Beach Motel.

Nearest town/resort: Holyhead

Out and about: An ideal location for touring the island of Anglesey with its many fine beaches and places of interest. Visit South Stack, a rock islet off Holy Island, with its precipitous cliffs, and famous lighthouse which is one of the most photographed landmarks in Wales. If you're feeling particularly adventurous, walk down the 360 steps and cross the narrow bridge to reach the new automatic lighthouse. Nearby are the remains of hut circles called Cytiau Gwyddelod, or Irishmen's Huts. Barclodiad y Gawres, 12 miles to the south west, is a megalithic tomb. A cruciform passage grave, it was raised in Neolithic times and has been excavated and restored. Aberffraw, 14 miles to the south-west, is the ancient capital of the kingdom of Gwynedd. Llywelyn ap Iorwerth, 'Llywelyn the Great', held court here, as did Llywelyn ap Gruffydd, 'Llywelyn the Last'. The sea zoo at Brynsiencyn on the banks of the Menai is well worth a visit, and purely out of interest you may wish to call at Llanfairpwllgwyngyllgogerychwyrndrobwll-llantisiliogogogoch. In the southeast corner of the island, Beaumaris Castle is a must for castle lovers, whilst Penmon Priory with its dovecote, and St. Seriol's Well, are also worth visiting. Santes Dwynwen is the patron saint of Welsh lovers.

She sleeps peacefully on Llanddwyn Island near Newborough, and the island can be reached on foot at low tide.

The pub, A to B: Take the shortcut by leaving the Park by way of the 'back entrance'…From the crossways near the reception area and toilet block follow the roadway that leads off in the direction of the sea. After 150 yards, when you run out of caravans, follow the path across the open field for another 300 yards to Porth Diana Lane and Ravenspoint Road. Now turn to your right and walk along for a further 400 yards to the *Seacroft Hotel* on the left hand side. You can enjoy the friendly atmosphere of the bar whilst sampling a pint of their guest ale. From the Seacroft to the end of the beach in Trearddur Bay is another 350 yards. When you reach here turn off left and follow the path along the beach for 500 yards to the far end. Turn left onto Lon Isallt for 150 yards then take the second turning on your right up to The Trearddur Bay Hotel - 100 yards away. Retrace your footsteps from the The Trearddur Bay Hotel back along the seafront to Ravenspoint Road. Turn to your left for 100 yards then right into Lon St. Ffraid and you will find The Old London Road Inn on your left. You've now covered roughly 1½ miles from start to finish - with the walk home still in front of you. So if you think this is too much walking for the one time you can always leave out part of the itinerary for again.

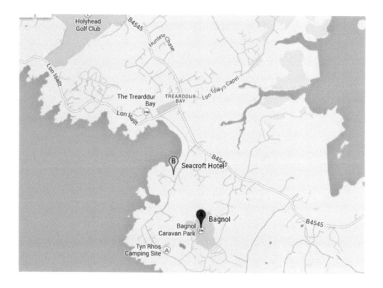

A. Bagnol to B. Seacroft Hotel

Epilogue

Whether you mean using this guide in whole or in part to help plan your touring adventure I sincerely hope you derive just as much enjoyment from your experience as I did whilst compiling the book.

Yes, I have very fond memories of the places I visited…the people I met…and the ales I sampled! And I'm sure you will too!!

As they say in Wales ~ Diolch yn fawr

As they say in Ireland ~ Go raibh maith agat
As they say in Scotland ~ Tapadh leibh

Thank you

Clive Williams

33464683R00057

Printed in Great Britain
by Amazon